FRIENDS AND LOVERS

Cultivating Companionship and Intimacy in Marriage

Joel R. Beeke
Cruciform Press | Released February, 2012

D1231488

To Mary, the WMWW,
my best friend, whose price is far above rubies;
in her tongue is the law of kindness (Proverbs 31).
– Joel R. Beeke

CruciformPress

© 2012 by Joel R. Beeke. All rights reserved.
CruciformPress.com | info@CruciformPress.com

"A book about love, marriage, and sex from Joel Beeke that is surprisingly candid yet without a trace of smuttiness. Putting Puritans in a new light perhaps, Beeke manages, at the same time, to be theologically thorough and pointedly practical. Fresh and refreshingly straightforward, **this is the best book of its kind.**"

Derek W H Thomas, Minister of Preaching and Teaching, First Presbyterian Church, Columbia SC; Distinguished Visiting Professor of Systematic and Historical Theology, Reformed Theological Seminary; Editorial Director, Alliance of Confessing Evangelicals

"Marriage is hard work. And wonderful. And sometimes, it's both at the same time. *Friends and Lovers* is **like a personal mentoring session on marriage** with a man whose heart is devoted to seeing Christ honored in how we love each other as husbands and wives. It's full of practical wisdom and grace. A delight."

Bob Lepine, Co-Host, *FamilyLife Today*

"By laying the theological, emotional, social, and spiritual foundations of marriage before heading to the bedroom, Joel Beeke provides a healthy corrective to the excessive and obsessive sex-focus of our generation and even of some pastors. Thankfully, he also goes on to provide **wise, practical, down-to-earth direction** for couples wanting to discover or recover physical intimacy that will both satisfy themselves and honor God."

Dr. David Murray, Professor of Old Testament and Practical Theology, Puritan Reformed Theological Seminary

"After years of marriage some of us still have to pray, 'Father, forgive me for my sins against those who love me the most.' We never stop needing counsel to better nourish and cherish those who are flesh of our flesh, our co-inheritors of the grace of life. **There is no better book than this** to renew the affection of happy marriage."

Geoffrey Thomas, Pastor, Alfred Place Baptist Church, Aberystwyth, Wales

"Central to the historical account of the creation of the human race is the marriage of Adam and Eve, their marriage being utterly vital to God's purposes for humanity. The pure delight our ancient parents had in each other, touching every aspect of their lives together, was sadly lost at the fall. What this book powerfully shows through the teaching of the Scriptures, though, is that this delight is recoverable to a great degree in Christ. Christian marriages should know a depth of intimacy, in all the best senses of that word, which other marriages do not have. It is a matter of sadness that some do not. Here, the biblical wisdom about marriage in these pages can help enormously. A mini-addendum: I appreciated enormously the way in which the divine gift of human sexuality is handled, with **biblical honesty but without any pandering to our culture's prurient ways**."

Michael A.G. Haykin, Professor of Church History and Biblical Spirituality, The Southern Baptist Theological Seminary

"Recently, a number of well known teachers have published books on marriage, some of which have caused quite a stir among Christians. Although these books offer some helpful insights, some are marred by an imbalance and even unbiblical teaching. Dr. Beeke's book, *Friends and Lovers: Cultivating Companionship and Intimacy in Marriage*, introduces biblical sanity into the discussion. With characteristic piety, scriptural knowledge, and practical guidelines, Dr. Beeke sets before us these two essential ingredients (friendship and intimacy) for a durable and happy marriage. This book **will strengthen the marriage of everyone who reads it**. I know it has mine."

Joseph A. Pipa Jr., President, Greenville Presbyterian Theological Seminary

Table of Contents

Friends and Lovers: Cultivating Companionship and Intimacy in Marriage

Print ISBN: 978-1-936760-44-2
ePub ISBN: 978-1-936760-46-6
Mobipocket ISBN: 978-1-936760-45-9

Published by Cruciform Press, Adelphi, Maryland. Copyright © 2012 by Joel R. Beeke.
All rights reserved. Unless otherwise indicated, all Scripture quotations are taken from:
The King James Version. Italics or bold text within Scripture quotations indicates
emphasis added.

Preface
REKINDLE THE FIRE

What once was a blazing fire has cooled into a smoldering heap of ashen coals. But if you blow gently upon the coals, you can rekindle that fire. Shave thin slices of wood off a dry log, gently pile them on the coals, and blow on them. Soon, flickers of flame will reward your efforts. Now carefully place small sticks of pine over the burning shavings. After they catch, add larger pieces of wood one at a time, pausing periodically to blow more air on the fire. Then smile as the flames mount higher. The fireplace will soon blaze and crackle.

Marriages can be like that fire. What once blazed hot now smolders faintly. The fire has not gone out, however, and the coals may retain their heat for some time. But the marriage is no longer warmed by the blazing fire that was there at first.

I am writing to tell you that God can rekindle the fire in your marriage.

Some people would say that the fire of marriage is the pleasurable intimacy of sex. Others would say that the fire is the companionship of dearest friends. In reality, both are true. Hand in hand, face to face, body to body, and heart to heart—marriage aims at *intimate companionship*. God gave us a picture of this grand aim when he made the first woman out of the man's side. When Adam saw her

he exclaimed, "Bone of my bones and flesh of my flesh!"
The two became "one flesh" (Genesis 2:23, 24). It was a
perfect match.

God intends for a husband and wife to walk together,
talk together, work together, and sleep together. Matthew
Henry famously said the woman was "not made out of
his head to top him, not out of his feet to be trampled
upon by him, but out of his side to be equal with him,
under his arm to be protected, and near to his heart to be
beloved." He then added, "See how dear the affection
ought to be between husband and wife; such as there is to
our own bodies (Ephesians 5:28)."[1]

Sadly, sin and death entered the world, and with it
came shame, blame, and power games within marriage
(Genesis 3:7, 12, 16). The relationship that was once the
fairest blossom of paradise is now a rose with thorns. The
sins in our marriages pierce our hearts. But thorns and all,
marriage still remains a fragrant flower worthy of desire.
We were not made to be alone. So how can we keep the
hearth fire of marriage burning?

By nature we are ignorant of what true love and
marriage should be, but Christ our prophet offers us
guidance in the Bible. We are guilty of dishonoring
marriage through our disobedience towards the God
who designed it, but Christ our priest shed his blood for
the forgiveness of our sins and now intercedes for us. We
are rebels without the strength to overcome the evil that
distorts and disrupts our human relationships, but Christ
our king conquers sin and rules us by his mighty Spirit,
making all things new—including our marriages. God

our creator is also our redeemer. The divine lawgiver who cursed us for our disobedience has sent forth his Son to redeem us from the curse of his law (Galatians 3:10–14, 4:4–5). God sent his Son to save sinners. He is the mediator who brings his people back to God and leads them once more in the paths of righteousness.

God's ultimate goal in saving us is far greater than just saving our marriages. One day Christ will raise up all believers and summon us to a wedding feast, the likes of which we have never seen. What a day it will be when we are face to face with him! On the way to glory, however, God transforms us in every area of life. Our submission to the heavenly Bridegroom requires doing his will today as husbands and wives.

This book aims to help you rekindle the flames of love in your marriage by the grace of God. If your marriage is still burning cheerfully, I hope it will help your love burn even brighter and hotter.

This little book is not a comprehensive marriage manual, nor is it a complete exploration of the theological significance of marriage. Instead it focuses on two key ingredients in a vital marriage: *friendship* and *sexual intimacy*. Drawing from the wisdom of the Bible, especially the book of Proverbs, I hope to help you grow closer to your spouse both emotionally and physically.

I dedicate this book to my dear wife Mary, the WMWW (world's most wonderful woman), who has given me untold joy in nearly a quarter of a century of marriage. I love her far more than words can ever express and thank God every day for her. Thanks, too, to our children, Calvin, Esther, and Lydia, who have been a joy to raise and haven't given any gray hairs to their parents.

May the Spirit of God blow upon your marriage through the Word of Christ so that smoldering coals of love may burst once more into flame, and may the fire of love be refueled to produce marriages that blaze with love to the glory of God!

✻ ✻ ✻

This book grew out of two addresses I gave at a conference sponsored by the National Council of Family Integrated Churches in Asheville, North Carolina, on October 28, 2011. I am grateful to Scott Brown and the leaders of NCFIC for the invitation to speak and for their warm, gracious hospitality. It was a blessing to be among them. I also thank Rev. Paul Smalley, Rev. Ray Lanning, Phyllis Ten Elshof, and Kevin Meath for their work in assisting me with this book.

Part One: Friends
COMPANIONSHIP IN MARRIAGE

There is a friend that sticketh closer than a brother.
— Proverbs 18:24

This is my beloved, and this is my friend.
— Song of Solomon 5:16

Introduction

Next to new life in Christ, close friendship in marriage is life's greatest gift. I am privileged to be engaged in a number of ministries, but friendship with my wife is worth more to me than any of them. Her friendship is priceless to me.

There's something deep and mysterious about this bond of Christian friendship because it reflects the very nature of God. We might define it as *the personal bond of shared life*. By this I mean something that joins two people together for a time. Friendship does not have to last for a lifetime to be true friendship, but the bond of true friendship typically takes months to build and lasts for years. It is not an accidental connection; it is a mutual bond of faithfulness. The highest form of such a bond here on earth is the lifetime covenant of marriage between a man and woman.

Friendship is not just any bond or relationship, but a bond of *shared life*. Deuteronomy 13:6 makes a passing reference to "thy friend, which is as thine own soul." This implies that losing such a friend would be like death. Your lives are so bound together that whatever touches your friend touches you.

Friendship is like the force that holds together the nucleus of an atom. It is an intimate bond that holds us together when other forces would push us apart. The stronger the friendship is, the closer its intimacy. R. C. Sproul writes, "In modern usage the term *intimacy* suggests merely a sexual relationship. But the word goes deeper than that. In its broad meaning, intimacy moves beyond the external and the superficial and penetrates the innermost dimensions of our life."[2]

As a bond of shared life, friendship brings our hearts and minds together in harmony. You might work closely with someone who has a very different mindset than you, but you are not likely to be friends. Friendship requires kindred spirits—that is, hearts and minds on the same wavelength. After a time, you may not even need to speak for a friend to know what you are thinking. You are like two strings on a well-tuned guitar: when one is plucked, the other string vibrates in harmony.

In choosing a marriage partner, we should seek such harmony. We want commitment, companionship, and closeness. We want to be best friends.

True friendship is as precious as it is rare. Indeed, the concept of friendship has become quite shallow today. For many people, "friends" are mere acquaintances or people you have "friended" on Facebook. Frankly, many people are so busy making money and entertaining themselves that they have little time for real friendships. The relational networks of our culture are breaking down even as our opportunities to communicate multiply through electronic media. In cyberspace we are awash with superficial connections and conversations, yet, in reality, many people are very lonely.

When it comes to human relationships, nothing is more tragic than loneliness in marriage. It is certainly possible to live in the same house, have joint bank accounts, and sleep in the same bed without being true friends. On the other hand, long ago Puritan Thomas Gataker (1574–1654) said, "There is no society [relationship][3] more near, more entire, more needful, more kindly, more delightful, more comfortable, more constant, more continual, than the society of man and wife."[4] By the grace of God, such friendship between husbands and wives is possible and practical and should be our priority.

Few books on marriage include even one chapter on friendship. But with God's help, we will first consider the foundation of friendship in marriage; second, how to cultivate friendship in marriage; and third, the temptations of friendship in marriage.

1: REMEMBER

The Foundation of Friendship in Marriage

Marriage was instituted by God at the dawn of human history. Both the sweet possibilities and bitter tragedies of marriage are rooted in the Bible's description of God's dealings with our first father and mother in Genesis 1–3. In Genesis 1:26, the Lord said, "Let us make man in our image, after our likeness." The divine image in man is the reflection of the divine "us" — that is, the three persons of the Godhead, one in substance and equal in power and glory, living together in unity and eternal love. The three persons constantly commune with one another and cooperate as one God in all they do (John 5:19–20). At the same time, as they work together, they subordinate themselves one to another in love. The Son delights to do the Father's will, and the Spirit delights to glorify the Son. This is beyond our comprehension, but by faith we believe that authentic friendship in Christ is rooted in the relationship of the three Persons of the Trinity with each other.

The triune God has chosen to display his glory in our common humanity, our gender differences, and our relationships with each other. "So God created man in his own image, in the image of God created he him; male and female created he them" (Genesis 1:27). There is but one humanity, shared by both men and women as creatures made in the image of God; yet there are two sexes, male and female, each distinct from the other, and both essential to human reproduction. Genesis 2 reminds us that without woman, man would be alone and bereft of companionship: "It is not good that the man should be alone" (verse 18). A search of the animal world revealed that there was as yet no creature fit to stand alongside the man as his companion in life and work. So God created woman — and man met his match!

As different as male and female are, they are united in marriage on the basis of their common humanity. "Marriage is honorable in all" (Hebrews 13:4), but it is not marriage per se: there is an added dimension to Christian marriage, for Christians are to marry only in the Lord. The partnership of two becoming one actually includes the Lord as a third party. Any definition of such marital friendship must then include the words *in Christ*; true marital friendship is *the personal bond of shared life in Christ*. Moreover, where husband and wife love and serve the same Lord, we see an earthly tri-unity that reflects the Trinity in heaven. The bond I feel with my wife, by which we two are one in the Lord, has helped me to know God better. It has helped me understand just a bit more how God can be three persons in one essence.

The purpose of marriage is more than emotional satisfaction or the fulfillment of physical desires. Married persons living together in love as heirs of the grace of life glorify God who is a community of three divine persons who share love, communication, cooperation, and their very essence. Alan Dunn says, "Marital intimacy is something more wonderful than mere biological mechanisms or animal urges…. Our inclination to intimacy is essential to our being: we are creatures made in the image of God."[5]

God's intent for marriage is clarified in the way he created woman. In Genesis 2:18, we read, "And the LORD God said, It is not good that the man should be alone; I will make him an help meet for him." He then showed the man that no mere animal would fit that description. Man's well-being depended on having a companion who could come to his aid in time of need and unite with him in doing God's will in the world. He needed someone "meet," or suitable, to who and what he was. This was a true friend.

So the Lord formed woman out of man's side. Genesis 2:23–25 says,

> And the man said, This is now bone of my bones, and flesh of my flesh: she shall be called Woman, because she was taken out of Man. Therefore shall a man leave his father and his mother, and shall cleave unto his wife: and they shall be one flesh. And they were both naked, the man and his wife, and were not ashamed.

This is a remarkable description of God's design for marriage, which includes oneness, separation into a special and unique relationship, mutual commitment to one another, and total openness.

Sadly, our first parents fell into sin, and their corruption had dire effects on their marriage. We see this in Genesis 3. Paradise ended even before the man and woman left the Garden of Eden; the loss of original righteousness severed their relationship with God and damaged their marriage bond. Their openness gave way to shame and guilt, so they covered their nakedness with aprons of fig leaves. As for mutual commitment, when God confronted them, the man tried to shift blame to the woman, knowing full well that the penalty of sin was death. God told the woman that the result of her sin was that her desire would be to conquer her husband, but that he would continue to rule over her, resulting in conflict, anger, and bitter estrangement. If you wonder why friendship in marriage can be difficult, the short answer is "original sin."

But God also showed grace to the couple. In Genesis 3:15, God declared that he would turn the hearts of the woman and her offspring against the devil. One day a descendant of the woman would crush the serpent's head and by his redemptive suffering bring deliverance to fallen mankind. They believed God's promise, so the man gave his wife a new name. He did not call her "mother of the dead," though death was now due to the race because of sin. Instead, he essentially repented of having blamed her for his own sin by calling her "Eve; because she was the mother of all living" (Genesis 3:20). He blessed her with a name of hope. He used his authority over woman to bless her, not to curse! By calling her "mother," he also recommitted himself to her as his wife and the mother of their

17

children. Thus, by the grace of God revealed in the gospel, their relationship as husband and wife was renewed.

We learn from the first three chapters of the Bible that friendship in marriage has a theological foundation. Married persons are to be friends in the best and deepest sense of the term. Such friendship glorifies the triune God by realizing the full, God-given potential of the marriage bond. Marriage is rooted in the basic facts of our creation; we were made to have communion with each other, and the closest possible communion is that between husband and wife. The beauty of this communion was marred by the Fall and obscured by the curse of sin, but friendship in marriage can be restored and renewed by faith in the promise of a Savior.

2: NOURISH

The Cultivation of Friendship in Marriage

The word "cultivation" is rooted in farm work. Seed is sown, and tender plants spring up, but they cannot flourish if they are not cultivated. Cultivation is rewarding work, for it results in an abundant harvest when God gives the increase. But it is hard work. Nobody wakes up one morning and is pleasantly surprised to discover that without any effort on his part, a field of ripe corn has appeared on his property.

Likewise, cultivating friendship in marriage is hard work, yet most rewarding. Many people in our culture think that love is something you fall into and therefore can easily fall out of. That might be true of passing emotions, but true friendship relies on cultivation: uprooting bad attitudes, planting daily seeds of love towards one another, pulling out weeds and eliminating pests that threaten to choke the relationship, watering the tender plants with daily prayer, and then taking time to reap a harvest of love and enjoyment in each other's company.

We must resist the laziness and ingratitude that often creep into marriage. Before you were married, didn't you invest a lot in each other? You couldn't wait to be together, and you made time for each other. You sent each other notes and talked often on the phone together. You paid each other compliments, brought each other gifts, gave each other hugs, and shared each other's daily joys and trials. If you stop doing such things after you marry, what will happen to your friendship? The tender plant of friendship will languish and die away. Friendship does not persist, deepen, and grow automatically.

What often happens is that married people begin to take each other for granted. They go their separate ways in the face of the pressures of work and the multiplying responsibilities of maintaining a home and providing for children. Instead of becoming more interdependent, a husband and wife become more independent. Before they know it, they wake up six years later and say, "Who is this person lying beside me in the bed?" The commitment may still be there. You still say, "I love you," and mean it. In fact, people can go on this way for years. But what happened to your friendship?

In Song of Solomon 5:16, the bride says of her husband, "This is my beloved, and this is my friend." On one level, that verse reveals the beautiful love between Christ and his bride, the church. But on another level, it shows how our marriages should mirror Christ's bond with his church. What a blessing to be able to say of your spouse, "This is my beloved, and this is my friend."

Friendship has many aspects, but what is common to all of them is *sharing*. Another word for friendship is *fellowship*, which comes from the Greek word *koinonia*. We tend to think of fellowship as drinking coffee and eating cookies with other people from church. But the word actually means *sharing* or communing with each other: sharing each other's joys, bearing each other's burdens, and being involved in each other's lives. Fellowship is one of the goals of the gospel. First John 1:3 says, "That which we have seen and heard declare we unto you, that ye also may have fellowship with us: and truly our fellowship is with the Father, and with his Son Jesus Christ." As members of the body of Christ, we are bound together in faith and love by the gospel of reconciliation. The same gospel should increase our love for each other as husband and wife as well as our longing to have fellowship with each other.

Let us explore several aspects of cultivating friendship in marriage under the theme of sharing.

Sharing Yourselves

The Lord describes his closeness with his people in terms of friendship. Exodus 33:11 says, "And the LORD spake unto Moses face to face, as a man speaketh unto his friend." God is a Spirit (John 4:24), so this verse does not refer to physical closeness or seeing any physical form or face of God. It refers to an immediacy of Spirit to spirit. God sent messages to his other prophets in dreams and visions, but he spoke his Word directly to Moses (Numbers 12:6–8). In the new covenant, this kind of spiritual intimacy is extended to true believers who yearn to walk with God (Ephesians 2:18, 3:12). God compares this closeness to what friends should be to each other: "as a man speaketh unto his friend."

John 15:15 tells us that Jesus said, "Henceforth I call you not servants; for the servant knoweth not what his lord doeth: but I have called you friends; for all things that I have heard of my Father I have made known unto you." Christ's words remind us that sharing ourselves is the heart of friendship. We must love each other as Christ loved us. Ephesians 5:2 says, "And walk in love, as Christ also hath loved us."

A woman once told me that when her husband was gone for four or five hours, she would ask him, "Where were you? What did you do?" He would say, "I don't ask you what you did today, do I? Don't ask me what I did today." A man who treats his wife that way has a servant in his house, not a friend. Jesus says friendship is not just giving commands but sharing what is on one's mind and heart. Richard Baxter (1615–1691) described this kind of sharing marriage:

> It is a mercy to have a faithful friend, that loveth you entirely, and is as true to you as yourself, to whom you may open your mind and communicate your affairs, and who would be ready to strengthen you, and divide the cares of your affairs and family with you, and help you to bear your burdens, and comfort you in your sorrows, and be the daily companion of your life, and partaker of your joys and sorrows.[6]

When you marry, the Lord says you enter into a covenant of companionship. Malachi 2:14 says, "the wife of thy youth" is "thy companion, and the wife of thy covenant." You promise to walk together all the way through the pilgrimage of life. Two practical ways to do that are spending time together and talking with one another.

Time. There is no substitute for spending time together. You are not a friend to your spouse if you work so many hours that you never have time together. Gary Smalley spent three years interviewing more than thirty happy families with very diverse geographic, social, and economic circumstances but with two specific things in common. First, they had "a concern for togetherness." They avoided doing too many activities that required them to be apart from each other. Second, they loved camping.[7] Now, maybe the thought of campfires and sleeping under stars thrills you, or maybe the daddy longlegs in the camp bathroom are more than you can handle! The point is: do things together.

Friendship cannot be warmed up by thirty seconds in the microwave. So much today is instant, but friendship is not. It costs something. It costs you yourself, your commitment, and your vulnerability. There are no rush orders in friendship. It must be baked slowly, gently, and continually if we want the flavor we are looking for.

Talk. One aspect of sharing your minds and hearts is discussing major decisions together and waiting until you have unity before moving ahead.[8] Any decision that significantly affects your time or money, or that involves a major change for your family's life, home, work, or church, should be made only after talking together about it, praying together, and coming to a point of unity. Although the husband is the head of the household, a godly man should not—with rare exceptions—lead his family against his godly wife's desires. As William Gouge (1575–1653) said, "Though the man be as the head, yet is the woman as the heart."[9]

To cultivate sharing yourselves, you must listen to each other. Be a good sounding board when your spouse needs to talk. Husbands, I will directly address you here because men in general are not known for their superior listening skills. When your wife says, "Honey, I feel this way," do you say, "Do this or that, and you will get over it"? She will most likely say in response, "I didn't ask you to tell me what to do. I just wanted you to know how I felt." Understand that your wife wants you to listen to her feelings and affirm them.

If you are a good listener, you can listen to your wife for twenty or thirty minutes about her concerns, and she may be satisfied even if you offer her no solutions. That doesn't mean your wife never needs counsel. But more often, she just wants to know that you are there for her. She wants to connect to you. So share yourselves with each other.

Sharing Your Faith

The deepest fellowship is spiritual fellowship, in which you share your life with a dear friend in the presence of the living God. It is remarkable how so few Christians actually enjoy spiritual fellowship with their spouses. I'm not talking about having family devotions, though that is a crucial spiritual discipline. I'm talking about sharing your faith with each other.

Obviously, to do this requires that you both have a living faith in Christ. Paul warns us in 2 Corinthians 6:14, "Be ye not unequally yoked together with unbelievers: for what fellowship hath righteousness with unrighteousness? and what communion hath light with darkness?" Spiritual fellowship is impossible unless Christ lives in both people in a marriage. For this reason Paul says in 1 Corinthians 7:39 that if a woman's husband dies, "she is at liberty to be married to whom she will; *only in the Lord.*"

If you are a Christian who is single, do not enter a romantic relationship with a person who does not love the Lord Jesus Christ and is not walking with God. Don't settle for someone who goes to church but has a questionable profession of faith. The minimum standard for dating or courtship should be a faith in Christ that is producing good works through love.

If you are a Christian and are married to an unconverted person who is willing to live with you, do not leave your spouse (1 Corinthians 7:12–13). But do not try to nag your spouse into the kingdom! Be the best husband or wife that you can possibly be so that you might win your spouse's heart with your godly conduct (1 Peter 3:1–2). Similarly, if your spouse professes to be saved but resists talking about spiritual things, give yourself to private prayer and serve your spouse with true love.

But if you are both Christians, then share your spiritual experiences. Share your spiritual concerns, frustrations and triumphs, your pilgrimage and your progress. Talk about how the Lord is working in your life by his Word and Spirit.

A pastor will sometimes visit a mourning widow and ask, "Do you believe your husband was a child of God?" Too often the bereaved says, "Seriously, I don't know; he never spoke about it. He read a lot, he went to church faithfully, he was serious, he was a good example, but he never shared one thing with me." How devastating! The most important part of life is faith in Christ Jesus, yet your partner knows nothing about it? Please don't be that way; share your spiritual struggles and hopes with your spouse.

Most importantly, share your faith as a couple by praying together. I realize that praying out loud can be intimidating for some Christians, and we should be patient with each other in this. But there is nothing like spending time in prayer each day as a couple, offering thanksgiving together for the day's blessings and petitioning God for the grace you need. Moreover, don't put off prayer if your spouse asks you to pray together at some point during the day when you don't normally pray together. Men, put down the book, set aside your tools, turn away from the screen, and pray. Women, turn off the stove, put down the phone, and pray. Baxter said, "It is a mercy to have so near a friend to be a helper to your soul."[10]

Sharing Your Trust

The traditional wedding vow includes the phrase, "I plight thee my troth," which means "I pledge my trustworthiness and fidelity to you." We need more "troth" in our marriages. Proverbs 18:24 says, "There is a friend that sticketh closer than a brother." Cultivate with your spouse a commitment that is more intimate and enduring than blood relations. Superglue your hearts together in an unbreakable bond.

Don't be a fair-weather friend. Before you married, you probably lavished gifts and attention on each other. But will you keep your troth when the fervor of first romance wears off? The Proverbs tell us that "wealth maketh many friends…and every man is a friend to him that giveth gifts" (19:4, 6). Let your spouse know through consistent faithfulness that you can be relied upon in good times and bad. Wives, don't be resentful if your husband's job takes him away from you more than you like. Husbands, don't be disappointed if your wife isn't as slim and cheerful as she was before having three children. Don't give way to such resentments. Don't make comparisons or covet other people's mates. Keep your hearts open to each other so that when your spouse wants to talk to you, you won't respond with a deaf ear or a critical spirit.

Trustworthiness nurtures trust. Trust develops over time as your relationship matures. You trust each other more and more as you learn to feel comfortable and confident with each other. Both of you should refrain from flirting with members of the opposite sex and should offer no reason for suspicion. Over time you should be drawn together in a deeper sense of troth, which binds you in friendship. You will feel comfortable when you see each other. That is what happens in a good marriage.

It can be like a pair of shoes. Don't take the parallel

here too seriously, but let me admit that I don't like shopping for a new pair of shoes. I much prefer slipping into my comfortable old shoes that fit so well. Most new shoes are too hard to break in! A good marriage, like a favorite pair of shoes, includes the wonderful, warm, cozy feeling of trust that builds over years in a marriage. Even more importantly, your mind and heart are at ease with who your spouse is and who you are when you are apart from each other. That is how a good marriage should be. You know deep down that your partner would do anything for you if you asked. That is true friendship.

So whatever you can do to cultivate mutual openness and confidence to build a sense of trust will build your friendship. Let me warn you here against things that tear down trust. First is lack of discretion and confidentiality. If your partner does not keep your secrets, trust will erode. Your friendship and maybe even your marriage will be destroyed. Proverbs 17:9 says, "He that repeateth a matter separateth very friends." To make yourself vulnerable in marriage, as you are called to do, you must be able to fully trust your partner not to tell your secrets to another person, such as a mother-in-law or friend at work. This is disastrous.

You should also be slow to believe rumors that you hear about each other. Rumors are very divisive, even if they have no basis in fact. Proverbs 16:28 says, "A froward man soweth strife: and a whisperer separateth chief friends." I'm not suggesting that you ignore any signs that your spouse may be involved in a sinful behavior. There are times when a wayward spouse must be confronted—if need be, with the help of your pastor. But realize that gossips don't care about the truth as much as the poisonous pleasure of speaking evil. You can't take seriously all that you hear, especially when it is contrary to what you know about a person's character and conduct.

Proverbs 31:11–12 says of a virtuous woman, "The heart of her husband doth safely trust in her, so that he shall have no need of spoil. She will do him good and not evil all the days of her life." Strive to be worthy of the trust that every man should place in his wife, and indeed every wife in her husband as well.

Sharing Your Joy

If you have a sour disposition, you will not cultivate friendship in your marriage. Whining, complaining, and otherwise ventilating your negativity are all forms of murmuring, which is condemned in Scripture as serious sin. A sense of humor, smiles, warmth, and optimism are important ways to encourage each other as best friends. So develop a joyful spirit. Proverbs 17:22 says, "A merry heart doeth good like a medicine: but a broken spirit drieth the bones." Laughing together is a sweet way to refresh your spirits and draw closer together.

Your children and your own human foibles should provide plenty of material for humor. Of course, God, sin, heaven, and hell are not laughing matters; we must never respond to such truths of God with levity. But there is much in life that we should not take so seriously. Learn to laugh at situations that are not inherently weighty. It's a way of saying, "The Lord is with us despite our idiosyncrasies."

Cultivate joy that does not depend on physical circumstances. Be of good cheer. Proverbs 15:15–17 says, "All the days of the afflicted are evil: but he that is of a merry heart hath a continual feast. Better is little with the fear of the LORD than great treasure and trouble therewith. Better is a dinner of herbs where love is, than a stalled ox and hatred therewith." If you have each other's love and fear the Lord, you can feast on inward joys even if you have nothing but peanut butter sandwiches for supper. Lead your family in giving thanks for all of God's blessings, even in hard times.

Learn also how to please your spouse. We read in 1 Corinthians 7:33–34, "But he that is married careth for the things that are of the world, how he may please his wife," and "she that is married careth for the things of the world, how she may please her husband." Pleasing someone (without compromising your faith) is a mark of friendship. Baxter wrote, "When husband and wife take pleasure in each other, it uniteth them in duty, it helpeth them with ease to do their work, and bear their burdens; and is not the least part of the comfort of the married state."[11]

Don't be so super-spiritual that earthly things don't matter. Wesley said that cleanliness is next to godliness, and he was not far off the mark. Personal hygiene is a must when two people live in close proximity. Grooming and dress are also important. Find out what your husband or wife likes, and do it. And avoid, as much as possible, doing things that displease your spouse. When my wife and I first married, I thought I was a careful driver, but my wife saw it differently. What to me seemed a safe distance between my car and the one ahead to her seemed danger-ously near. I had to be willing to sacrifice my ideas about driving in order to make her feel safer in the car with me. Since her feelings about this were much stronger than mine, it was only reasonable that I should be the one to yield. Baxter said, "Avoid therefore all things that may represent you unpleasant or unlovely to each other…. whatever is loathsome in body or mind, must be shunned as temptations which would hinder you from that love, and pleasure, and content, which husband and wife should have in one another."[12]

To please your spouse, you must know him or her, and a big part of knowing your spouse involves your spouse honestly telling you what is pleasing or displeasing to him or her. One man early in his marriage was asked by his wife if he liked the meal she prepared. He hated it, but he was afraid to offend her, so he said it was good, and he ate that meal once a week for the rest of his life. Is that kind of deception a recipe for friendship in marriage? Be honest with one another about your likes and dislikes. That will help your spouse love you.

Sharing your joys also means sharing activities that you both enjoy. Look for areas of common interest and invest in them. If your spouse enjoys something that is not your favorite activity, learn to enjoy it. Go along to an event, and even if you can't appreciate it, enjoy his or her enjoyment. The more your lives overlap, the closer your friendship will become. Of course, all things must be subject to the glory of God. I am not suggesting that you make an idol out of leisure activities—for example, skipping church to go hunting together. On the other hand, if you are so busy with church and school that you never have time to go to a concert or have a picnic, you are missing out on pleasures God wants you to receive with thanksgiving and enjoy.

3: RESIST

The Temptations of Friendship in Marriage

By reason of sin, the friendship of a husband and wife does not go unchallenged. We face many pitfalls that could injure our marriage. In God's providence, these challenges may provide us opportunities to grow closer to God and closer to each other. The word *temptation* can mean a situation that incites us to sin or a heaven-sent test to strengthen us. Let's consider how we should respond to three temptations and turn them into opportunities to grow. Rather than addressing obvious temptations like abandonment or adultery, I will focus here on more subtle temptations in marriage.

Avoiding Correction

Our worst faults are usually plain to everyone but ourselves. These faults should be addressed, but everyone is reluctant to do so. Sadly, we are much more prone to give advice than to receive it, but the wise counsel of a friend can bring us joy.

Counsel beautifies us. Proverbs 27:9 says, "Ointment and perfume rejoice the heart: so doth the sweetness of a man's friend by hearty counsel." Think of this, wife: when your husband gives you loving counsel, he is anointing your soul with the sweet fragrance of Christ.

Good counsel also sharpens us so we may serve the Lord better. Proverbs 27:17 says, "Iron sharpeneth iron; so a man sharpeneth the countenance of his friend." Husband, remember this: when your wife gives you wise counsel, she is sharpening the blade of your soul to a razor's edge so that you become a powerful weapon for the Lord.

The most difficult type of counsel is correction, yet Proverbs 27:5–6 says, "Open rebuke is better than secret love. Faithful are the wounds of a friend; but the kisses of an enemy are deceitful." Best friends are honest with each other. You may have acquaintances with whom you never argue, but they are not good friends because you seldom speak the truth in love to each other. My wife or either of my brothers could criticize me, and I wouldn't be offended because I know they love me. We need friends like that, and we especially need such spouses.

You can cultivate the ability to take criticism from your spouse or give it without offending the other by what I call "the sandwich principle." You lay down a slice of bread, as it were, by saying something like, "You are wonderful and I appreciate you in so many ways." You then name some ways that especially please you. Then you lay down a slice of meat, saying, "But I am really concerned about one thing. I feel like you don't seem to care about how my days go, you seldom ask me about them, or, when you do, you don't seem interested in listening to my answer." Then you put down the other slice of bread and say, "Don't get me wrong, I am not criticizing you as a person. I am just criticizing one particular thing. I still love you very much, and you still have so many wonderful qualities." When you do that, your partner will be more inclined to eat your sandwich.

This is not manipulation; it is disciplined thankfulness. Jesus handled several of the seven churches of Asia this way in Revelation 2 and 3, as did Paul in most of his epistles written to various churches. What happens too often when we criticize someone is that we accompany it with strong, negative feelings. We criticize without ever mentioning how many other things we appreciate about our spouse. We fail to be thankful to God for the many good things our spouses bring into our lives. If I come to my wife and simply say, "You don't care about me or how my days go," she might respond by saying, "Wait a minute! Look at all the things I do for you—and, by the way, you don't seem to care so terribly much about how my days go either." There is a vast difference between wise counsel and selfish complaining. Let us share counsel with humble gratitude.

But, you may ask, how should you respond to a spouse when honest communication and constructive criticism lead to nothing but a blow-up and a scolding? "What, you don't like my cooking?" "You don't trust me when I am away at the office?" "You expect me to spend more time with in-laws who hate me and insult me?" "Why do I have to spend every moment of my free time tagging along wherever you decide to go, doing what you want to do, having no life of my own or time to myself?"

"Talking about this only makes me angry. It doesn't help me get over it."

Great wisdom and patience is needed to handle such responses with love. Don't overreact. Remember, not all spouses respond equally well to constructive criticism. Some lash out quickly because their feelings are hurt. If you are patient, however, and don't respond in kind, refusing to render evil for evil but instead listening carefully and thoughtfully, most spouses will calm down within a short period of time. If you persist in reassuring your spouse that you love him or her, your spouse may even soon apologize for blowing up or scolding you.

Whatever the case may be, get to know your own spouse, and learn to respond to his or her responses in effective and helpful ways.

Imbalance in Other Relationships

When you get married, your spouse's family becomes your family. You may suddenly have four parents instead of two. The commandment to "honor thy father and thy mother" (Exodux 20:12) applies to all four parents. So love them, respect them, serve them, listen to their counsel, and support them in their old age. Loving your in-laws will go a long way in building friendship with your spouse.

At the same time, establish yourselves as a distinct family unit. Remember that Genesis 2:24 says, "Therefore shall a man leave his father and his mother, and shall cleave unto his wife: and they shall be one flesh." Marriage creates a new family unit. Parents are no longer your primary support and sounding board; your spouse comes first. You may still seek the advice of parents or in-laws, but go to them as a couple, not on your own.

Do not speak evil of your in-laws either. Husbands, if your wife makes a critical comment about her father or mother, do not add a criticism of your own, for you may discover later that your wife is angry with you for what you said! You must honor your spouse's parents. Never put down your in-laws, even if your spouse does so.

Nor should you ever speak evil of your spouse in front of your parents or your in-laws. That could deeply hurt your spouse. Speaking evil includes making jokes that tear a person down: kidding can do serious harm. Correct your spouse in private and consistently honor your spouse in public.

Relationships with in-laws are the subject of many jokes, but in reality, these relationships are great opportunities for building friendship with your spouse. In making an effort to love, honor, and bear patiently with the faults of your in-laws, you show love for your spouse. You are saying to your spouse, "I love you; therefore, I will love the people who are an important part of your life."

Some parents will try to intrude far too much in the lives of their married children or make unreasonable demands on their time and attention. Such cases are best dealt with by the son or daughter—not the son-in-law or daughter-in-law. The son or daughter should then speak with his or her parents, verbalize how much those parents are loved, and then explain the situation so that a clear agreement of expectations can be reached.

Likewise, our relationships with brothers and sisters can build our relationship with our spouse, even as we must consider relationships with siblings as a lower priority than our relationship in marriage. Proverbs 27:10 says, "Thine own friend, and thy father's friend, forsake not; neither go into thy brother's house in the day of thy calamity: for better is a neighbor that is near than a brother far off." Certainly your spouse should be closer to you than any brother or sister. As precious as sibling relationships can be, a husband or wife must come first.

In all extended family relationships, seek to maintain a loving balance. Don't shut out the rest of the family, but don't get enmeshed in their affairs either. Make sure that you spend a reasonable amount of time with both sides of the family.

Within your circles of friends, give priority to your marriage, but don't discount the importance of other friendships. Some couples are so madly in love that they think they don't need anyone but each other, but God designed us to enjoy a network of relationships. He calls the church a body, in which the members have organic relationships with many other parts. So don't be jealous if your husband or wife has a good friend of the same sex, or even a limited working relationship with a person of the opposite sex. As much as is appropriate, make friends with your spouse's friends. Do not consider them as "my friends" or "my spouse's friends" but as "our friends."

On the other hand, do not spend so much time with your friends that your marriage suffers. There is something wrong if a married person wants to spend two or three nights a week with people other than his or her spouse. Your earthly relationships should be like a set of concentric circles: marriage is on the inside; children next; then your parents, siblings, and close friends and church family; and on the outer circle, cyber friendships developed on-line and other acquaintances. Never allow an emotional attachment outside of your marriage to overshadow your relationship with your spouse. That can be the first stage of adultery. Make your husband or wife your best friend.

Personal Crises

A friend is someone you can trust to be there when you need help, especially when you need spiritual help. Galatians 6:2 says, "Bear ye one another's burdens, and so fulfill the law of Christ," and the verse prior to this speaks about restoring people who have fallen into sin. A big part of bearing each other's burdens is offering spiritual support to someone who has fallen into sin and needs to be restored. So when your spouse succumbs to tempta-tion, don't rush to condemn: pray! First John 5:16 says, "If any man see his brother sin a sin which is not unto death, he shall ask, and he shall give him life for them that sin not unto death." Pray that your spouse would come to repentance, be forgiven by God, and be strengthened to fight against such temptations in the future.

Perhaps the most powerful form of spiritual support is forgiving each other. Jesus said your prayers won't go far unless you forgive (Matthew 6:14–15). Peter warns husbands that if they fail to live with their wives "according to knowledge, giving honor unto the wife," their prayers will be hindered (1 Peter 3:7). Arrogance and bitterness will turn your marriage into an empty shell. Your spouse may hurt you deeply. Remembering that forgiveness is not identical to trust—for trust takes time to build—you must forgive your spouse. That means releasing all claims to punish him for his past sins, to demand restitution, or to seek revenge.

When you forgive your spouse, you demonstrate the gospel through your actions. You can also experience the gospel more powerfully in your own life. In forgiving from the heart, you remember your own sins and God's forgiveness toward you. Ephesians 4:31–32 says, "Let all bitterness, and wrath, and anger, and clamor, and evil speaking, be put away from you, with all malice: And be ye kind one to another, tenderhearted, forgiving one another, even as God for Christ's sake hath forgiven you."

In addition, help each other bear emotional and physical burdens. Job 6:14 says, "To him that is afflicted pity should be shewed from his friend." When Job was in deep distress, he cried out, "Have pity upon me, have pity upon me, O ye my friends; for the hand of God hath touched me" (Job 19:21). The best thing Job's friends did was sit with him, weep with him, mourn with him, and keep silence with him for seven days (Job 2:11–13). The worst thing they did was open their mouths to blame Job for his troubles (see Job 4 and following).

A true friend is the opposite of an acquaintance, who moves in to take advantage of you or gets in your way to thwart you; a true friend gets in your way when you are falling to lift you up and support you. More than this, to support your spouse means that you don't exaggerate his faults. Maybe burned toast is such a little thing that you shouldn't even bring it up. Why bother? Eating four hundred pieces of burned toast isn't so bad. Or is it? You must make that assessment yourself. How willing are you to suffer being wronged in this way? Some people complain about every discomfort to the point of being ridiculous. Appreciate your spouse's positive points and support each other. Let the small things go.

The trouble is that when you get very close in marriage and some faults keep reappearing, you soon tend to exaggerate the faults of your spouse while becoming blind to your own. "I'm being reasonable, but she's being ridiculous!" It is said that "rare is the person who can weigh the faults of others without putting his own thumb on the scales."

The greatest support a spouse can give is to be with you when you most need it. Proverbs 17:17 says, "A friend loveth at all times." Be such a friend to your husband or wife! Stand with your spouse through thick and thin. You are showing to the world the faithfulness of the Lord.

Conclusion

Friendship in marriage is a gift from God. As we saw from Genesis, it originates in the nature of God and expresses itself in us as creatures made in his image. Therefore, a good friend should be cherished. Pray for friendship in Christ, and seek God's blessing on your marriage so that your spouse would be your best friend on earth. And when God grants that request, give him thanks.

At the same time, don't expect too much of this or any other friendship. Be realistic. Your spouse is not God. Friendship with your spouse cannot meet all your needs or ensure that your marriage will be trouble-free. Your spouse is not sinless, nor are you. You will have to bear with faults and foolishness all your days together.

If, however, you find that, despite your prayers and best efforts, your friendship in marriage has degenerated largely into acrimony or even hatred, go to a wise Christian counselor sooner rather than later. Should your spouse refuse to go with you, go alone. Marriage is too important to let acrimony rule instead of friendship. Too many married people wait too long to seek help for marriages in which friendship is weak. It is far better to seek counsel too early than too late.

Finally, remember that ultimately we stand alone before God. Neither your wife nor husband nor any other friend can stand in for you in your relationship with God. You are responsible to him for "the things done in [your] body" (2 Corinthians 5:10). Even if you try to ignore the Lord, he is still there, always watching and always working. Every other person is of no significance in comparison to him.

A man with three friends was charged with a serious crime and summoned to court. He went to his first friend for help, but all the friend could offer was a nice set of clothes to wear to his appearance before the judge. The man went to his second friend, but that friend could only accompany him to the entrance of the courtroom. The third friend not only went with the man all the way into court but pled his case so well that he was acquitted and set free.

That is a parable for us all. We could say that a dying man has three friends. The first friend is his material wealth. All this friend can offer is a suit to be buried in. The second friend represents dear ones on earth who love him, who can only accompany him to death's door. But the third friend is the Lord Jesus Christ, who is with us through life and death. He will plead our case in heaven so that we are counted righteous by God. He is the greatest friend that we and our spouses can ever have!

Part Two: Lovers
SEXUAL INTIMACY IN MARRIAGE

My son, attend unto my wisdom, and bow thine ear to my understanding: That thou mayest regard discretion, and that thy lips may keep knowledge.... Drink waters out of thine own cistern, and running waters out of thine own well. Let thy fountains be dispersed abroad, and rivers of waters in the streets. Let them be only thine own, and not strangers' with thee. Let thy fountain be blessed: and rejoice with the wife of thy youth. Let her be as the loving hind and pleasant roe; let her breasts satisfy thee at all times; and be thou ravished always with her love.

—Proverbs 5:1–2, 15–19

Introduction

The gospel of Christ energizes us to enjoy sex as a sacred passion. The gospel I refer to is the good news that God's Son died for sinners, taking the punishment that his people deserved, and then rose from the dead, offering eternal life to all who repent of sin and trust in him alone. The gospel offers all people, whether single or married, present joy and future blessing beyond our deepest imagination. But for married people, the gospel also motivates us to make sacred love.

This may surprise you. The root of much sexual dysfunction is a lingering doubt whether marital sex is pure and acceptable in God's sight. In some ways this dysfunction is much like what someone might say about a piece of double chocolate cake: "It tastes so good, it must be sinful." Do you sense how perverse the statement is — that good things are sinful?

Paul warns against this mindset:

Now the Spirit speaketh expressly, that in the latter times some shall depart from the faith, giving heed to seducing spirits, and doctrines of devils; Speaking lies in hypocrisy; having their conscience seared with a hot iron; Forbidding to marry, and commanding to abstain from meats, which God hath created to be received with thanksgiving of them which believe and know the truth. For every creature of God is good, and nothing to be refused, if it be received with thanksgiving: For it is sanctified by the word of God and prayer. (1 Timothy 4:1–5)

If we believe that it is wrong to enjoy God's creations such as food or marital sex, then we believe a lie of the devil. All things are to be received with thanksgiving as the good gifts of a loving Father in heaven. However much the gifts of God may have been abused, perverted, and corrupted in the world, for the Christian they are cleansed and made holy again by truth of the Word and the power of believing prayer. Paul says in 1 Timothy 6:17 that the opposite of materialism is not asceticism but putting our hope "in the living God, who giveth us richly all things to enjoy."

Sexual love in marriage is like fire in a fireplace. If the fire breaks through the boundaries of the fireplace and ignites other parts of the house, it can destroy your property, kill your family, and end your life. Likewise, sex outside of its God-ordained boundaries destroys and kills. What the world considers sexual freedom is really death. "Whoso committeth adultery with a woman lacketh understanding: he that doeth it destroyeth his own soul" (Proverbs 6:32). But we would not want to harbor such a fear of fire that we could never again enjoy the dancing flames in a fireplace. A blazing hearth is warm and beautiful. Likewise, sex within marriage is a warm and beautiful way to be close to the one you love.

Christianity does not forbid or frown upon sex. Nor was sex rediscovered by archaeologists in the 1960s after centuries of being locked in a church basement. Vibrant sexuality is part of our Reformed heritage. It is true that in the Ancient Church and in the Middle Ages, the church generally frowned upon sex, glorifying celibacy even in marriage. Indeed, marriage was usually viewed as a mere concession to human weakness.[13] The church forbade sex on holy days and sacred seasons, which, based on the crowded medieval church calendar, made sex with one's spouse a sin for more than three-quarters of the year.[14] Ironically, this led to glorifying sex and romance in the context of adultery. You could either be holy with the Virgin Mary or have fun with wicked Jezebel. The Protestant Reformation of the sixteenth century brought people back to a biblical view of sex as God's creation within marriage.

The Puritans also taught the importance of a good sex life within marriage.[15] More than that, they celebrated romantic love. Leland Ryken writes,

> Throughout the Middle Ages, love poetry and love stories had celebrated adulterous romantic love. By the time we reach the end of the sixteenth century, the ideal of *wedded* romantic love had replaced the adulterous courtly love ideal of the Middle Ages as the customary subject for literature. C. S. Lewis

47

has shown that "the conversion of courtly love into romantic monogamous love was… largely the work of English, and even of Puritan, poets." Someone else claims that the Puritans "did what courtly lovers had never dared to do; by combining the romantic love relation and the marriage relation, they created the new social institution of romantic marriage."[16]

Indeed, the Reformed and Puritan tradition has a healthy, God-glorifying, marriage-honoring perspective on sexual intimacy in marriage. Matthew Henry (1662–1714) wrote of being "always ravished with the love of a faithful virtuous wife."[17] In biblical thinking, passion and purity go together. Sex becomes the beautiful and noble crown upon a godly marriage.

But how does the river of human sexuality, poisoned by our Fall, polluted and disgusting, become a clear stream of refreshing water through the gospel of Christ? The gospel is not just the gateway into the Christian life or a ticket to heaven; it must be central to the entire Christian life. As Paul says in Titus 2:11–12, "For the grace of God that bringeth salvation hath appeared to all men, Teaching us that, denying ungodliness and worldly lusts, we should live soberly, righteously, and godly, in this present world." Therefore, the gospel is central to Christian marriage; it trains us to forsake sin and to live rightly towards our spouse. Paul's teaching on marriage in Ephesians 5 is full of the gospel.

According to the Bible, sex is an important part of marriage. God designed it so when he created man and woman. Sex is part of the created order, sustained by his common grace. Since the created order is fallen, however, sin has deeply wounded us at the point of our sexuality, as part of the totality of our depravity. But praise God for the gospel, for by it, grace heals fallen nature. The gospel teaches us to receive the gift of sex in marriage as God's gift to us, to be used for our good and for his glory. All humanity, not just Christians, can enjoy the emotional and physical benefits of sex within marriage. For helpful advice from a Christian perspective, I recommend Ed and Gaye Wheat's book *Intended for Pleasure*.[18]

Let's consider nine ways (sections 4 through 12) in which making love to our spouses can glorify God and bring the promise of great blessing for Christians.

4: CHERISH

Sex Is the Act of Cherishing Each Other as God's
Image-Bearers

Sex starts in the kitchen, as the saying goes. That
means that what happens in your bedroom is in many
ways determined by how you relate to each other
throughout the day. Sex does not *make* a good marriage;
it is the *fruit* of a good marriage. Husband, the way you
treat your wife at the breakfast table may well affect your
wife's response to you at night in the bedroom, even if you
can't remember what you said about the pancakes.

Humans cannot treat sex as a mere physical act in
isolation from the rest of life, as though it is a mere animal
instinct. Genesis 1:27 says, "So God created man in his
own image, in the image of God created he him; male and
female created he them." Our gender and sexuality are
dimensions of an entire person created in God's image.
So sex is not just about genitals and hormones. Human
sexuality is the coming together of two people—male
and female—who were made to serve God and love one
another. The best sex springs from a relationship in which
we honor each other throughout life.

This implies that sex should never degrade or demean

a spouse. While the Bible does not go into detail about what kinds of sexual activity are permissible, it does make clear that we should not engage in sex in a way that treats someone like a slave, an animal, or an object. Sex should always communicate honor to a person in a way that is appropriate to God's image-bearer. The Heidelberg Catechism (Question 108) puts its finger on essential values of the Christian life—purity and holiness—when it says that the seventh commandment teaches us to detest all uncleanness, and "live chastely and temperately, whether in holy wedlock, or in single life."

Scripture furthermore implies that sex thrives in an environment of personal communication. Men and women were made in the image of God as a result of communication among the three persons of the Godhead, all of whom agreed to the proposal, "Let us make man in our image." So too husbands and wives must talk with one another in a spirit of agreement for their physical relationship to flourish. Gary Chapman writes, "Sexual intimacy is the result of a relationship, and relationship is fostered by communication…. If we do not have time to talk, then we don't have time for sex."[19]

The Bible often refers to sex using the biblical idiom "to know" your spouse. For example, Genesis 4:1 says, "And Adam knew Eve his wife; and she conceived, and bare Cain." While this word for sex does not always imply a relationship,[20] it does imply that sexual intimacy grows in the context of mutual knowledge and commitment.[21] If you believe that your spouse is God's image-bearer, then you will want to know her, cherish her, and care for her, much as you long to know God and express your love for him. Sex is part of knowing your spouse.

Peter says in 1 Peter 3:7, "Likewise, ye husbands, dwell with them according to knowledge, giving honor unto the wife, as unto the weaker vessel, and as being heirs together of the grace of life; that your prayers be not hindered." We must treat our wives with honor and respect as fellow human beings and, if they are believers, as fellow children of God. At the same time, we are called to remember how different our wives are from us and not put them down for their weaknesses; rather, their differences are just another reason to honor them.

Forgive me for stating the obvious, but women are quite different from men. Men generally have a higher metabolism, less body fat, more muscle, and stronger bones than women. Their hearts and lung capacity in proportion to their weight is larger than that of women. Women, on the other hand, have stronger immune systems than men. At the same time, their bodies are generally more sensitive and responsive to touch, taste, smells, and sounds.

The difference between men and women is also social. A study of 250 cultures showed that males are almost always the rule makers, hunters, builders, weapon makers, and forgers of metal, wood, and stone. Women are consistently most involved in raising children, caring for the home, and preparing food and clothing. They are also more skilled at reading people's emotions and relationships.[22]

The differences between men and women show up most powerfully in marriage. A husband and wife approach their relationship differently, with different desires and goals. Psychologist Willard Harley has described these differences well, although his book *His Needs, Her Needs* gives the false impression that if you do not meet your spouse's needs, your marriage is doomed to end in adultery and/or divorce.[23] In reality, godly people have faithfully endured bad marriages while finding deep joy and comfort in Jesus Christ. But if we aim to love each other, we cannot ignore the desires and longings of our spouse.

We must never forget that our deepest desires and needs are for God and can only be met by God. Nonetheless, the more we seek to satisfy a spouse's desires, the deeper our sexual intimacy will grow and honor God. Harley's book offers some suggestions that can help us think about how to love our spouses. These are generalizations, so apply them as you learn how to best serve your spouse.

Husbands, honor your wives. A wife's primary desires from her husband usually include leadership, affection, conversation, appreciation, trustworthiness, financial support, and fatherly commitment to the children. So husband, don't expect your wife to respond to your sexual advances if you give her little time beforehand for personal conversation, especially telling her how much you love her and appreciate her work around the house. She might say to you, "Honey, I love your hugs, and I love your kisses, but what I need right now is help with the dishes." C. J. Mahaney advises, "Touch the heart and mind of your wife before you touch her body."[24]

If you touch her heart often through kind words and trustworthy deeds, you most likely will be delighted to discover what happens when you do touch her body.

Husbands and wives, be sensitive to each other's desires. Men also need to understand that the sexual experience of a woman is somewhat different from that of a man. Both men and women want sex. However, as Chapman points out, men tend to have more of a physical drive towards sexual intimacy whereas women tend to have more of an emotional drive towards sexual intimacy. A man is visually aroused by the sight of his wife, whereas a woman is aroused by such things as tenderness, thoughtfulness, talking, touching, and time spent together. Men often want to move quickly towards a sexual climax, while women move more slowly.[25] These are general-izations, of course, for a husband's needs for emotional intimacy can be every bit as great or even greater than his wife's and a wife's physical desires for sex can be every bit as great or even greater than her husband's, but the point is that you should learn how your spouse operates and work together for mutual satisfaction.

Wives, respect your husbands. A husband has a strong desire for a wife who gives him companionship, sexual fulfillment, submissiveness, attractiveness both in body and soul, admiration, domestic support, and motherly commitment to their children. So wives, you might be surprised how much more attractive you would appear to your man if you frequently praised him for his accomplishments at work. You might say, "What does that have to do with sex?" It has everything to do with sex, because sex is not just a physical act but one dimension of a relationship between two people created in God's image.

Perhaps it would be good after this section to sit down as a couple and ask each other, "What do you most deeply desire from me and our marriage? How can I do a better job of serving you that way?" Sex is a relationship between two people in God's image.

5: MULTIPLY

Godly Lovers Delight in Multiplication

Sexual intimacy ordinarily goes hand in hand with bearing children. Having created man, male and female, in his own image, God says, "Be fruitful and multiply" (Genesis 1:27–28). If we truly see human beings as the image-bearers of God, we will want to see his image-bearers multiplied on earth. If you try to enjoy sexual intimacy with your spouse while despising the thought of bearing children, then you are tearing apart what God joined together. As so many have done, you will pervert your own sexuality and sexual identity. Whether or not God gives you children depends on his sovereign will. Perhaps he will use you to bless children not of your union. But the most sexual husband has the character of a father, and the most sexual wife has the heart of a mother.

Birth control is an important issue in many marriages. There is no way I can do that subject justice in this space, but here are a few basic guidelines: first, we must push back against our culture's obsession with "family planning." To agree upon a marriage for our own selfish ends where my spouse and I will only have two or three children, and for all the rest of my wife's child-bearing years we will simply use some means of birth control, is a far cry from fulfilling the biblical mandate to be fruitful and multiply (Genesis 1:28). Such an attitude smacks of arrogance, lack of faith, and an unwillingness to submit to the will of God who opens the womb (Psalm 113:9). We must never forget that we do not have children just for our own sake, but also for the church and the nation. God is greatly glorified through large covenant families who serve and fear him.

Second, using natural methods of birth control for some months directly after a wife has delivered a child, or when a wife is plagued with medical or psychological conditions that warrant it, is nowhere condemned in Scripture. Husbands in particular must exercise some measure of leadership and wisdom in this regard. I know of a husband who lost his first wife to an early grave because he would not consider using birth control, yet insisted on having sex with his wife even after her doctor had warned that another pregnancy would be fatal. This is human irresponsibility and folly, not courageous faith. A husband must also recognize how much his wife is able to cope with. Some women can handle having eight or nine children well, but for others that would simply be overwhelming.

Third, any means of birth control that would involve the possibility of destroying life must be rejected outright as sin and murder in God's sight. There is a difference between methods that prevent conception and those that abort a conception that has already taken place.

Finally, though my wife and I personally have

never felt free in our consciences to use any kind of
artificial birth control, I have no authority to say that
every Christian couple must follow our example. Rather,
Christian couples should prayerfully and carefully study
the Scriptures, consider the evidence, and then determine
the will of God for them in this situation. It is critical,
however, to arrive at this decision not from a purely
selfish perspective but from a divine perspective. True
faith seeks to know and do the will of God, and to do all
things to God's glory.

But is the possibility of producing offspring the only
reason married couples should enjoy sex? No, sexual
intimacy should continue after your bodies can no longer
produce children. Sex functions as God's gift for our
companionship and pleasure into our older years. Until
then, to engage in willful rebellion against God's call to be
fruitful and multiply is wrong and harmful to your own
sexuality.

6: OBEY

Sex in Marriage Is Obedience to God's Commandments

God commands you to make love regularly with your spouse if it is physically possible. Obviously, medical problems can make this impossible — at least for a time, and sometimes permanently. But when health permits, regular, physical, sexual intimacy is the will of God for married couples. If that were not clear enough from the words "they shall be one flesh" in Genesis 2:24, we have the express declaration of 1 Corinthians 7:3–5:

> Let the husband render unto the wife due benevolence: and likewise also the wife unto the husband. The wife hath not power of her own body, but the husband: and likewise also the husband hath not power of his own body, but the wife. Defraud ye not one the other, except it be with consent for a time, that ye may give yourselves to fasting and prayer; and come together again, that Satan tempt you not for your incontinency.

The Greek words translated "due benevolence" communicate the idea of obligation, a debt that must be paid.[26] Richard Steele (1629–1692) wrote, "The sober use of the marriage-bed is such a mutual debt, that it may not be intermitted long without necessity and consent."[27] William Gouge (1575–1653) wrote, "As it is called benevolence because it must be performed with good will and delight, willingly, readily and cheerfully; so it is said to be due because it is a debt which the wife oweth to her husband, and he to her."[28]

The Creator has placed us under an obligation to love our spouses physically—with our bodies as well as with our souls. As a result, the husband and wife have power, or authority, over each other's bodies. Sex is not a privilege we may choose to grant for good behavior. If we withhold sex from one another as an act of power, we defraud and rob one another.

The only exception is setting aside brief periods of time for intense spiritual exercises such as fasting and prayer. Even this exception, however, is offered as permission and not a command (1 Corinthians 7:6). Though Paul recognized the advantages of being single for Christ, he also said people who marry are under divine obligation to have an ongoing sexual relationship with their spouse.

Sometimes the Christian view of sex is caricatured as negative. For example, how many times have you heard people mock marital sex as boring, as though spouses always say to one another, "Oh, honey, not now; I have a headache"? Indeed, that is the way some Christians view sex. But wisdom teaches us that to avoid fornication and adultery, a man and a woman who love each other in the Lord and seem fit for each other as marriage partners should marry and make love. The best way to prevent adultery is to have sex with your spouse. Matthew Henry said, "Mutual delight is the bond of mutual fidelity."[29]

This does not mean that one spouse has the right to demand sex every night regardless of how tired the other spouse is. Nor must a spouse demand a certain kind of sexual activity if the other is uncomfortable with it. Though the marital bed is "undefiled" (Hebrews 13:4), we must not fall prey to the notion that a woman must do whatever her husband wants her to do in bed. Moreover, even when there may be mutual consent, we should not engage in every form of sexual practice promoted in our sex-intoxicated culture. We should reject our culture's obsessions with increasingly bizarre and extremely weird forms of sex that seem to make sex an end in itself. The Heidelberg Catechism (Question 108) points out rightly that marriage is not a license to indulge in sexual practices of every kind. We should not discard the biblical commands to be chaste and temperate simply because we are married.

These objections notwithstanding, regular lovemaking is God's command to married couples. Someone might object, saying this makes sex a mere duty and not an act of love. It may seem to drain sexual intimacy of all romance and make it mechanical. My response is that duty does not exclude delight any more than obedience to the law excludes love. Love is the essence of the law, and true obedience to God means serving him with gladness (Psalm 100:2).

Proverbs 5:18–19 give us this remarkably strong counsel: "Let thy fountain be blessed: and rejoice with the wife of thy youth. Let her be as the loving hind and pleasant roe; let her breasts satisfy thee at all times; and be thou ravished always with her love." God calls us to enjoy each other's bodies passionately. This is not mechanical obedience; it is whole-hearted love. Gouge wrote, "As the man must be satisfied at all times in his wife, and even ravished with her love; so must the woman be satisfied at all times in her husband, and even ravished with his love."[30]

Tim and Beverly LaHaye wrote that this same passage in Proverbs "also indicates that such lovemaking was not designed solely for the propagation of the race, but also for sheer enjoyment by the partners."[31] We note that the text specifically refers to enjoying a woman's breasts, not just having genital intercourse. This suggests what today we call foreplay: caressing and kissing each other's bodies with pleasure prior to coitus.

So when we think about bedroom activities, we should remember that the gospel brings with it the law. The seventh commandment does not merely forbid adultery; by positive implication it requires "conjugal love, and cohabitation" among married couples, as the Westminster Larger Catechism (Question 138) reminds us.[32]

We have a sacred duty to give our sexual affection and our bodies to our spouses. Sexual intimacy is part of our gospel response to God's mercy described in Romans 12:1, "I beseech you therefore, brethren, by the mercies of God, that ye present your bodies a living sacrifice, holy, acceptable unto God, which is your reasonable service." If this command to offer your "bodies" to God as living sacrifices includes sex (as it must), then our highest goal in sex cannot be a better experience in sex itself but greater obedience to the Lord.

7: LIBERATE

Sexual Freedom Comes Through Forgiveness of Sins

Maybe you are thinking, "Great! I read this book for some advice on improving my sex life, but all you did was make me feel guilty." Dear friends, if the law of God makes you feel guilty, you were already guilty of breaking the law. But thanks be to God, the gospel does not merely repeat the law! The law of God brings us the knowledge of sin and the wrath of God (Romans 3:20, 4:15), but the gospel offers us the freedom of forgiveness.

Colossians 2:13–14 says, "And you, being dead in your sins and the uncircumcision of your flesh, hath he quickened together with him, having forgiven you all trespasses; Blotting out the handwriting of ordinances that was against us, which was contrary to us, and took it out of the way, nailing it to his cross." Here, "all trespasses" includes sexual sins. All the accusations of God's holy law were nailed to the cross. If you trust in Jesus Christ alone for salvation and righteousness, then you are totally forgiven.

You may need forgiveness for sexual sins committed against your spouse. You may be guilty of withholding sex when you should have given it freely. You may be guilty of using sex as an instrument to control or punish your spouse. You may have given your body but refused to give your heart, turning sex into a hollow and empty shell. Perhaps you gave your sexuality to someone other than your spouse or to the false intimacy of pornography and sexual fantasizing. But all of this guilt is nailed to the cross the moment that the Holy Spirit unites you to Jesus Christ with the bond of true faith. So confess your sins, repent of them, and rest in the promise of forgiveness.

Perhaps you feel guilty because you engaged in sexual sin before marriage. Whether it was sexual sin with the person to whom you are now married or with another party, guilt weighs down your conscience. Every time you approach the marriage bed, you bear a secret burden. You feel unclean. Sex seems dirty now because you made it dirty before.

Sometimes the guilt of previous sexual sins is the cause of present sexual problems. A woman may be cold to sex with the man she loves because she is paralyzed with guilt and shame over her past relationships. A man might struggle with impotency for the same reason. Their view of sexual intimacy in marriage is poisoned by the memory of past sins.

If this is so for you, listen to the promise of 1 John 1:9, "If we confess our sins, he is faithful and just to forgive us our sins, and to cleanse us from all unrighteousness." The blood of Christ can wash away all the dirt of the past (1 John 1:7). Using the power of Christ's blood shed for you on the cross, God will forgive your sins and cleanse you from all unrighteousness of body and soul.

You might still object, saying, "I know God forgives me. I just can't forgive myself!" If that is so for you, I ask you as gently as I can, are you not being arrogant? You are acting as if you can be judge of all the earth. Whose word determines whether a person is guilty or forgiven: yours or Christ's? Your problem is not that you need to learn to forgive yourself; rather, your problem may be pride. If so, you should humble yourself before the throne of grace and submit to God's Word, not your own judgment. If you continue to cast guilt upon your conscience for acts that God declares are forgiven, you need to examine why you are not submitting to God's Word and why you insist on burdening your conscience when God has already forgiven you.

God has given Christ the authority to forgive sins (Mark 2:10). We all need his forgiveness, especially regarding our sexuality. So as a needy sinner, rest your hearts in Christ. Return to him again and again for fresh infusions of a sense of his blood-bought forgiveness. Cling to the promise of Micah 7:19: "thou wilt cast all their sins into the depths of the sea."

8: RELY

Faith in Christ Empowers Sexual Love

The Christian life from beginning to end is driven by faith in Christ. Paul says in Galatians 2:20, "I live by the faith of the Son of God, who loved me, and gave himself for me." Do you believe that apart from Christ you can do nothing, but if you abide in him you will bear much fruit (John 15:5)? Do you apply that to sex? If a passionate sexual relationship with your spouse is God's will, then Jesus Christ can give you the full, sufficient grace to increasingly do God's will towards your spouse.

Sex should be one expression of your love for your husband or wife. Love is the fruit of the Holy Spirit (Galatians 5:22). We receive the Spirit's work by the continual act of trusting in Christ as he is revealed in the gospel (Galatians 3:1–5).

So here you are in the kitchen with your spouse, knowing that you will later head for the bedroom. You know that you are commanded by God to have sex with your marriage partner. You see how empty you are of true love. So your heart cries out, "Father, strengthen me with power by your Spirit so that Christ will dwell in me! Give me divine love, that I may love my dear husband or wife as I love myself." As you walk by faith in the path of obedience, you will experience Christ's power. Have you ever prayed for God to enable you to glorify him in the way you make love to your spouse? You can and you should.

Some people carry baggage into the bedroom. We have already talked about the burden of guilt and how Christ can lift it, but you may also carry the burden of corruption. You may approach sex with a mind clouded by lurid memories and images. Perhaps those come from your past. If you are looking at pornography, I plead with you to throw away the pictures in magazines or in digital files on the computer or on cable TV. If necessary, get rid of the technology that channels this garbage into your life. Christ tells us to be as radical in fighting against sin as a man who cuts off his own right hand to avoid temptation (Matthew 5:27–30).

Even after you do this, you can't delete your own memory files. You still feel polluted. You are aware that your approach to your spouse has been corrupted. Yet there is hope, dear friends. Again, I say, "Look to Christ." You once fixed your eyes on worthless things, but now fix your eyes on Jesus Christ. Christ has the power to purify your mind. As we behold his glory in the gospel, we too may be transformed from glory to glory (2 Corinthians 3:18). Feed your mind with meditations on Christ and his beauty, and he will enable you to put off the lusts of this earth so you may put on the graces of heaven (Colossians 3). Even if you are horrified to find an evil image or idea springing into your mind in the midst of making love to your spouse, let your heart cry out for mercy to Christ. Seek Christ on the marriage bed because you are there to do God's will.

9: GIVE

Sex Is More Loving with Self-Denial

Selfishness kills lovemaking. No matter how physically attractive a person is, he will provoke weariness and disgust from his wife if all he wants to do is take and never give. One key to good sex is going to bed as one called to serve. You do not exist for yourself; God made you to glorify him by serving others. Isn't that what the gospel teaches us through the example of Christ? He made himself a servant and then humbled himself (Philippians 2:6–8). He did not come "to be ministered unto, but to minister, and to give his life as a ransom for many" (Mark 10:45). What does this look like in a Christian marriage? In this section, we will consider practical applications for husbands and then for wives.

Christ is the model for husbands in loving their wives (Ephesians 5:25). So, husbands, before reaching for your wife, remember that you are called to give yourself up for her. Sexually, this means, as referenced before from C. J. Mahaney, that a husband must touch his wife's heart before he touches her body. But it also means that he keep touching her heart while he touches her body. Speak words of love to her. Praise her. And touch her body in ways that will touch her heart. Learn what she likes. Patiently give it to her. It might involve a lot of kissing or a backrub before you reach something explicitly sexual. But it will give your wife a much more profound sexual satisfaction.

I can hear the objection already: "But it takes my wife so long! How am I supposed to wait? I was born ready." It does seem that from puberty onwards, most men need very little preparation for a sexual experience. It may be, husbands, that you will have to wait, touching and talking, until your wife ascends the mountain peak and is ready to leap off with you and come floating down. Then, too, the time may come in later years, when the patience, talk, and tender touching of your wife will be needed to prepare you for sex. By taking time now to satisfy her, you are enlarging a retirement fund that you can withdraw from later. Regardless, your God calls you to obey now this command to love your wife, which in part means preferring her sexual satisfaction over your own.

It is precisely here that we are called to serve the Lord by faith. Remember Christ's call to discipleship in Luke 9:23–24: "And he said to them all, If any man will come after me, let him deny himself, and take up his cross daily, and follow me. For whosoever will save his life shall lose it: but whosoever will lose his life for my sake, the same shall save it." Making love is hardly bearing a cross. But making love, if it is truly an act of love, involves self-denial. And Thomas Watson (c. 1620–1686) said, "Self-denial is the sign of a sincere Christian."[33]

Christ promises that we will find life by dying to

ourselves. That doesn't mean you will necessarily get a better sexual experience that night. Frankly, there are some nights when denying yourself will mean no sex at all. Perhaps she is exhausted or desperately needs to cry on your shoulder. Maybe you need to make amends for the way you have mistreated one another and spend time rebuilding trust and emotional connections. A self-denying sex life will feed on a thriving spiritual life with God and a deepening relationship with your spouse. Ordinarily, your sex life will improve with your patience and understanding. You will not only enjoy your own pleasure, but you will increasingly enjoy each other's pleasure as well. But regardless of how your spouse responds—you can't control that completely—your soul will expand beyond the narrow confines of selfish sensuality and receive treasure in heaven. Watson wrote, "Frolicking sensualists live as if there were no world to come. They pamper their bodies but starve their souls."[34] It is better to deny your body for now and strengthen your soul for eternity.

Wives, your self-denial may look different from your husband's but it is no less real. In some cases a wife's sex drive may be stronger than that of her husband. But more commonly, wife, denying yourself may mean making yourself cheerfully available to your husband more often than you would otherwise choose. Maybe you are tired; busy mothers often are. Maybe you have a lot of emotions swirling around in your heart. Perhaps the husband of your youth is no longer your knight in shining armor—or at least his armor is getting a little rusty and dented! But one of the best ways you can strengthen your husband and affirm his masculinity is by making love to him.

Don't make love to your husband as if condescending to his weakness. Be thrilled that God has given you the power to please your man and serve him. Revel in his love for you. Enjoy him and enjoy his enjoyment of you. Discover what he likes and give it to him. Though women are less often the initiators in sex, feel free to initiate it when you want. Your husband may be greatly pleased by that. Use your feminine gifts of creativity and keen observation to make your husband a happy man.

Even as we speak of self-denial in sexual intimacy, we rejoice in the goodness of God's creation.

10: RESTORE

Our Father in Heaven Can Heal Fear and Shame

Naked. The very word evokes feelings of embarrass-
ment and shame. Ever since Adam and Eve reached for fig
leaves, we have wanted to cover up our nakedness. There
is something exhilarating about being naked with your
spouse, yet this is also a very vulnerable position. If this
is true of sheer nakedness, then how much more is it true
of the sexual embrace. We see either a remarkable sense of
acceptance and trust in the love of our spouse or a shatter-
ing experience of rejection. That is why sex can prompt fear.

Here too the gospel empowers us, for it contains the
assurance of being loved by God. Because of that love, we
are called by God to love others. Ephesians 4:32–5:2 says,
"And be ye kind one to another, tenderhearted, forgiving
one another, even as God for Christ's sake hath forgiven
you. Be ye therefore followers of God, as dear children;
And walk in love, as Christ also hath loved us, and hath
given himself for us an offering and a sacrifice to God for
a sweetsmelling savor." Paul keeps grounding our love for
each other on God's love for us. The more you know his
love for you, the more his love will cast out your fears and
empower you to love another.

I want to walk softly here, but surely this is part of healing for victims of rape, incest, or other forms of sexual abuse. In such cases, sex is associated with overwhelming darkness in your mind. Perhaps you have memories that torment you even though the crime occurred decades ago. Perhaps you even feel ashamed because even though your husband is a good man, you stumble every time you try to run into his arms. David Powlison writes, "The experience of violation can leave the victim self-labeled as 'damaged goods.' Sex becomes intrinsically dirty, shameful, dangerous. Even in marriage, it can become an unpleasant duty, a necessary evil, not the delightful convergence of duty and desire."[35]

I do not want to belittle your pain by being simplistic. But the love of our Father in heaven for you as a believer is so pure and powerful that knowing him can heal you. He may not wipe away all your tears until you see his glory face to face, but even now the Holy Spirit leads us into the ever-deepening experience of the fullness of God's love. So go deeper into the knowledge of the Father. Study the doctrines of God, election, and spiritual adoption, and bathe your mind in the truth about your Father in heaven. Cast away lies that you believed about him on the basis of your experiences. Pray for the Holy Spirit to teach your heart through Christ. And seek biblical counseling as needed.

Whether or not we had a traumatic sexual experience, we will find the strength to become vulnerable in sex in the assurance that God loves us eternally, richly, affectionately, and with absolute purity. You can help your spouse to discover God's love by being a living image of his acceptance in Christ. Make your sexual relationship a place of safety in an unsafe world.

11: REPENT

Sexual Idolatry Requires Repentance

Our worship of idols is closely linked to sexual sin, as Romans 1 and the history of Israel (e.g., Numbers 25) reveal. Many idols and false gods of the ancient world were associated with sex or fertility. But idolatry is not just a matter of bowing before a statue. It is rooted in being captivated by some created thing or person instead of the Creator. Colossians 3:5 teaches us that greed (or "covetousness") is a kind of idolatry.

Remind yourself that sex is good, but sex is not God. David Powlison writes, "Sex is a real but secondary good."[36] So it is acceptable to pursue sex but only as a means of honoring God, the creator of sex. If our marriage bed is to be a holy temple in which we offer ourselves as a living sacrifice to God, then we must cleanse it of idols.

Let me identify three idols, all based on lies and delusions, that can distort sexual intimacy.

- The idol of perfect beauty
- The idol of pleasure
- The idol of pregnancy or lack of pregnancy

The idol of perfect beauty. Long before Hollywood began to stamp the collective consciousness with an unrealistic definition of physical beauty, women—and to some extent men, as well—were concerned about their own attractiveness. But this concern has intensified greatly over the years. Today, body image is a big problem not only for women, but also for many men, as indicated by the growing prevalence of eating disorders cropping up among them. We no longer compare ourselves to the best-looking people in our town or school, but to supermodels who have the benefit of airbrushing, professional make-up artists, and personal trainers. Our cultural obsession for youthfulness as well as comparing ourselves to impossible standards of beauty can wreak havoc in the bedroom as it becomes an idol either for our lust or for our envy.

But physical beauty is of relatively little value in marriage, for God has given beautiful people no more ability to please their spouses, even in bed, than ordinary-looking people. Happiness in sexual relations should have little to do with the size and shape of your body, but a person's character has everything to do with it, for as Proverbs 11:22 warns us, "As a jewel of gold in a swine's snout, so is a fair woman which is without discretion." So press on in godliness, take care of your body, and give yourself to your spouse as you are without shame.

The idol of pleasure. Our pornographic society has severed sex from marital love and turned it into a superficial adventure in pleasure seeking. Sexual pleasure, especially the orgasm, has become another idol in our time. The world suggests that sex is an athletic event in which two people with perfectly conditioned bodies take the gold medal for achieving the most orgasms in the greatest possible number of positions with the greatest number of partners. In reality, people with so-called "perfect" bodies will be the worst lovers in the world if all they care about is themselves and their own pleasure.

By contrast, a husband and wife with very ordinary bodies can have very good sex because of the love, tenderness, and intimate knowledge they have for each other. Rather than treat each other like soulless beasts, they come together in romantic friendship and loving service to each other. R. C. Sproul says, "You are called to satisfy your husband or wife. You have only one standard to meet. Keep your eye on that and forget the superstars of sex."[37]

The idol of pregnancy or lack of pregnancy. A more subtle idol is allowing sexuality to be ruled by the desire for conception. That is what motivated Rachel to say to Jacob, "Give me children or else I die" (Genesis 30:1). A natural desire for children is a blessed motivation in sexual intimacy, but when having children becomes everything to us, then it ruins sex because we use our spouse and fail to glorify the God who alone can open the womb (Genesis 30:2). Pray for grace not to let childbearing become an idol.

It is also possible for pregnancy to become an idol of fear. Having a child might threaten your plans for the future. Or perhaps the thought of pregnancy raises the specter of miscarriage if you have lost children before.

Certainly some fear is understandable if you face a situation that could lead to much pain. But if this fear prevents you from drawing near to your spouse in sexual delight, it becomes an idol.

In reality, neither having children nor losing children nor going childless can secure or destroy our happiness. Only God can give us happiness. Beauty, pleasure, and children are also gifts from God: receive them with thanksgiving, but do not pursue them as if true happiness is found in them. Sex is not heaven, men are not gods, and no woman is a goddess; the greatest pleasures in life are hollow without God. We are fallen human beings with limitations.

Repenting of sexual idolatry can help us deal with sexual impotence or frigidity. Some of these problems have a medical cause, but they might also be the result of winding ourselves so tightly about some idol that we cannot relax. Fear, anger, and pride hinder sexual ability. So ask what dominates your heart and how this may displease the Lord. For example, you may be obsessed with pride in performance, whether at work or in bed. One failure may lead to another until failure in bed buries you even deeper. Here again, return to the gospel of our God's unmerited love and acceptance, which is mirrored for us in a loving spouse who accepts us no matter what. We should also humble ourselves and realize that marriage is about love, not about performing.

I have focused on sexual idols, but difficulties in the bedroom may also be fed by another kind of idol. Ask yourself what is going on in your heart. Are you angry? Afraid? Why? What do you want, and why do you want it so badly? How does that manifest pride and arrogance? Ask yourself these questions. Then pursue the wholehearted attitude of exalting the Lord and humbling yourself.

A strong dose of humility can make sex much more enjoyable. Instead of bearing the heavy weight of super-human expectations, we can just be ourselves. Indeed, we can laugh at our weaknesses when we are embraced in the arms of someone who accepts us unconditionally. How beautiful that is! In a climate of gospel-nurtured grace, we are free to enjoy God's gifts with our spouses without trying to make sex into something it was never designed to be.

12: APPRECIATE

Gratitude and Contentment Sweeten Sex

We read earlier from 1 Timothy 4:4, "For every creature [or creation] of God is good, and nothing to be refused, if it be received with thanksgiving." Later, Paul says that "godliness with contentment is great gain" (1 Timothy 6:6). So let us receive God's gift of sexual intimacy with thanksgiving and contentment. Gary Thomas writes, "Ironically, the idolatry of sex and obsessive guilt over sex accomplish the same thing—they keep the focus on self, whether it be out of enjoyment or despair. Gratitude, on the other hand, turns our hearts toward God."[38]

Grumbling is a grave sin against God. Philippians 2:14 says, "Do all things without murmurings and disputings." God gives us manna in the wilderness, but our sin makes us yearn for the fleshpots of Egypt. Remember how Israel's grumbling revealed wicked unbelief and even hatred against God, provoking his deadly wrath against an entire generation of Israelites? "Forty years long was I grieved with this generation…unto whom I sware in my wrath that they should not enter in my rest" (Psalm 95:10–11). Isn't God provoked when you complain about the spouse he has given you—not to mention your job, your clothes, your house, your daily bread?

Grumbling is a sin against God and against our spouse. Ingratitude focuses on the negative, essentially saying, "I wish my wife looked different" or "I wish my husband acted differently." Such thinking hinders us from truly enjoying our spouse. We withdraw our affections and then are offended when our spouse does the same. We become blind to our entrenched selfishness and cry out, "Give, give" (Proverbs 30:15). "You're not meeting my needs" has been trotted out in an effort to justify many a broken marriage. Behind it all is the pride that says, "I have the right to a certain kind of spouse or to a certain amount of sexual pleasure and gratification."

You have no right to anything except judgment for your sins. You deserve to be married to a devilish spouse and to lie down in a bed of flames. It is amazing how good God is in giving us anything good at all! Some marriages may break the heart and wound the soul. But when you see that you are a hell-deserving sinner, surely you must also admit, "I am receiving better than what I deserve." And if you have a believer for a mate, no matter how immature, you have cause to bless God every day.

Instead of filling out mental complaint forms against our spouses, let us fill our minds with lists of appreciation and gratitude. It might help you to write such things down. Gratitude applies to every aspect of marriage, including physical affection.

Hear again the words of Proverbs 5:19: "Let her breasts satisfy thee at all times; and be thou ravished always with her love." Breasts are mentioned here because most men find them sexually stimulating. Look for the things about your spouse's body that please you, and focus on them. Sexual excitement is, at least in part, an exercise of the mind. This is a good principle for your entire marriage, not just sex. Take the position that God brought this man or this woman to you "as with his own hand."[39] Married persons, Steele wrote, "ought to love each other with a superlative love; and when the sacred knot is once tied, every man should think his wife, and every wife her husband, the fittest for them of any in the world."[40]

Train yourself to focus exclusively on your spouse. Sunlight diffused abroad merely warms, but sunlight focused through a lens ignites a flame. So it is with marriage. Thomas says, "Marriage calls us to redirect our desires to be focused on one woman or man in particular rather than on society's view of attractive women or men in general…. On the day I was married [to Lisa], I began praying, 'Lord, help me to define beauty by Lisa's body.'"[41] Even more important, train your desires to respond to your spouse as a whole person. Bodies decay and die, while the souls of Christians go from glory to glory as they become more like Christ. When married persons focus their attention on each other, Steele said, "The thoughts, desires, and actions of each of them are confined to their own lawful yoke-fellow, as the dearest, sweetest, and best object in the world; and this by virtue of the covenant of their God."[42]

Do you think of your spouse as exclusively consuming

and delighting? The Hebrew word for being ravished is sometimes used of drunkenness (Proverbs 20:1, Isaiah 28:7), and so a husband should be "ravished always" (Proverbs 5:19) or " intoxicated always" (ESV) by his wife's love. It is a strange and wonderful thing that Scripture compares a sober and pure love with drunkenness!

Gouge recognized this and derived from it two applications that help us exercise gratitude and contentment with our spouse. First, just as foolish people or drunks are sometimes blind to real problems, you must intentionally turn a blind eye to your spouse's defects during sexual intimacy. Gouge wrote, "If a man have a wife, not very beautiful, or proper, but having some deformity in her body, some imperfection in her speech, sight, gesture, or any part of her body, yet so to affect her, and delight in her, as if she were the fairest, and every way most complete woman in the world."[43]

Second, just as foolish or intoxicated people have strong passions that lead them to act in passionate ways, let your passion be guided by love into such strong displays of affection that people know you are passionately obsessive about your spouse. Gouge said, "An husband's affection to his wife cannot be too great if it is kept within the bounds of honesty, sobriety and comeliness."[44]

One Puritan told his wife that his love for her was "a golden ball of pure fire." Another ended several letters to his wife with "sweet kisses and pure embracings."[45] Therefore husbands and wives, be playful and creative and intense in your affection for each other. Do not behave inappropriately, for "[love] doth not behave itself unseemly" (1 Corinthians 13:5)—which is, of course, where the parallel with intoxication breaks down. Nevertheless, know that you have God's seal of approval upon being "ravished" with the love of your spouse. It glorifies him, for it cultivates gratitude for his gift to you.

CONCLUSION

Sex in marriage is a great blessing from God. Gouge wrote, "This due benevolence…is one of the most proper and essential acts of marriage: and necessary for the main and principal ends thereof: as for preservation of chastity in such as have not the gift of continency, for increasing the world with a legitimate brood, and for linking the affections of the married couple more fitly together."[46]

So receive this gift from God, and freely give it to each other. Making love to your spouse fulfills good purposes. It guards you from adultery, it may produce children whom you can raise up as living images of God in the world, and it links your affections to your spouse in a marvelous way, contributing to true intimacy. Thank God for this gift!

As in all matters of personal sanctification, growth in sacred sexuality will take time. Do not think that now that you've read this book, you can stop learning. You are in the journey of a lifetime. An insight that God has given you may enable you to take a big step forward, but there will be more steps to take after that. See your sexuality as one dimension of growing into an entire way of life that will increasingly bring glory to our God.

Sex is not your life; Christ is your life. So pursue a healthy sexual relationship with your spouse in obedience to Christ. But if providence denies you sexual fulfillment, pour out your heart before the Lord and rejoice in him. Like marriage, sex is a temporary gift pertaining only to this life; Christ and his graces last forever.

Sex is not even the life of your marriage. A tree may be alive and fruitful and yet have one withered branch. This is not to contradict the commandments of Scripture to have sex with our spouses but merely to recognize that the sum of the law is love. If your attempts to enjoy sex together are replete with many difficulties, do not despair. Just love each other! As Thomas says, "Give what you have."[47] Entrust the rest to God.

Appendix
QUESTIONS TO PONDER

The alarm goes off, and as you look at the time, you freeze in disbelief. You have apparently hit "snooze" more times than you realized, and now you're late! You rush into the bathroom. Dressing in front of the mirror, you see a classic case of "bed head," a hairstyle somewhere between a bird's nest and a mushroom cloud. Just then your kids start arguing, and you rush out of the bathroom to adjudicate the dispute. Grabbing a cold muffin, you launch out the door and drive to work. After you get there, you sense a few stares and hear some snickers. *Come on,* you think, *it's not like nobody's ever been late before.* Then you remember that you did not deal with what you saw in the mirror and, in fact, totally forgot what you looked like. You head for the office restroom with comb in hand.

Reading this book can be like looking in a mirror. No doubt God's Word discussed and applied here to marriage has helped you see some neglected aspects of your life. The question is: what will you do about it? Will you just walk away and forget what you saw? James 1:22–25 says,

But be ye doers of the word, and not hearers only, deceiving your own selves. For if any be a hearer of the word, and not a doer, he is like unto a man beholding his natural face in a glass: For he beholdeth himself, and goeth his way, and straightway forgetteth what manner of man he was. But whoso looketh into the perfect law of liberty, and continueth therein, he being not a forgetful hearer, but a doer of the work, this man shall be blessed in his deed.

In the mirror of God's Word, perhaps you have seen some ways in which you are neglecting *friendship* with your spouse. Study this checklist and mark the items needing change:

- Should you repent of the way you have viewed marriage and have taken for granted your personal bond of shared life with your spouse?
- Are you investing in your friendship with the gifts of your time, thought, talk, tenderness, and touch?
- Are you opening your heart to your spouse, learning to trust him or her, and making important decisions by discussing things together?
- Do you talk with your spouse about how God is working in your life to make you more like Christ? Do you ask about your spouse's spiritual life, then listen graciously to the response?
- Do you pray and give thanks together every day, sporadically, or not at all?
- How committed are you to the exclusivity of your

relationship? How supportive are you of your marriage? Do you gossip about your spouse's secrets or flirt with members of the opposite sex?

- Are you cheerfully seeking to please your spouse in every lawful way? Does something you do annoy your spouse such that you should stop doing it?
- How do you respond when your spouse corrects you?
- Do you avoid correcting your spouse, correct harshly, or take the effective, biblical route and mingle correction with affirmation?
- Do you grieve your spouse in the way you handle relationships with your parents, in-laws, and friends? Is your marriage your top priority?
- Do you forgive your spouse's sins against you or do they make you bitter?
- Are you present for your spouse in times of crisis? Are you a friend who loves at all times, a sympathetic, compassionate, listening supporter?

Which points on this list did you mark as showing the need for change and improvement? Make a plan for how, with God's help, you will pursue the needed changes.

God's Word may also have reflected back to you an image of some ways the gospel can empower you to glorify Christ more as your spouse's *lover*. Here is a checklist for you to review regarding your sexual relationship with your spouse. Mark the categories where God's Spirit has convicted you of sin, and then discuss them with your spouse:

- Do you treat sex as an isolated, physical event or as part of a relationship fostered by loving communication and mutual service?
- Have you divorced sex from begetting or bearing children? Or have you coupled sex with a godly delight in multiplying God's image-bearers on earth?
- Are you obeying God's command to make love to your spouse regularly and willingly as health permits or are you rejecting God's authority over your sexuality?
- Have you found freedom from sexual guilt and shame by confessing your sins and trusting in the blood of Jesus Christ to wash and make you clean again?
- Do you look to Christ to purge your heart of sexual sins and fill you with love?
- Have you purged your home and your habits of enticements to sexual lust?
- Do you approach lovemaking as a servant, denying self in order to love your spouse?
- Is your sexuality hindered by fear and shame? Are you drinking deeply of the healing love of the Father as revealed in the doctrines of God, election, and adoption?
- Do your fears, frustrations, or desires about sex reveal an idol in your heart? If so, how are you acknowledging and enthroning God as your supreme Lord?
- Do you view sex with your spouse with an attitude of gratitude or of grudging? Do you accept your spouse as a gift from God?

As you finish this book, do not think that merely reading it will make you a better friend and lover. Go on to select a few points under each category of friendship and sexual intimacy, then in dependence on the Holy Spirit, resolve to pursue growth in that area. Remember that the Lord does not ask you to walk alone on the pathway of obedience. He will go with you as your all-sufficient, covenant-keeping God if you trust in his Son.

Approach your marriage, as all of life, with a God-centered perspective shaped by the five great *solas* (or "alones") of the Reformation: Scripture alone, grace alone, faith alone, Christ alone, and the glory of God alone. Reject any ambition to use marriage as a means to glorify a mere human, and live for *the glory of God alone*. Do not rely on your own understanding but follow *Scripture alone* as the rule of life. Do not be self-righteous or trust in the merit of your own works, but humbly receive and rest in God's gift of *justification by faith alone*. After committing to change and grow, do not depend on your own strength, but labor with prayer for sanctification by *grace alone*. And seek all blessings by looking to *Christ alone*. He is the mediator of all grace and the friend of sinners.

So go ahead; walk away from the mirror, but don't forget what you have seen. By the Spirit's grace, walk in the path of obedience as a married person, with Christ walking beside you both as your heavenly friend and the lover of your soul.

Endnotes

1. Matthew Henry, *Exposition of the Old and New Testament* (Philadelphia: Ed. Barrington & Geo. Haswell, 1828), 1:36 [on Genesis 2:21–25].

2. R. C. Sproul, *The Intimate Marriage: A Practical Guide to Building a Great Marriage* (Phillipsburg, NJ: P&R Publishing, 2003), 13.

3. Archaic term for "the quality or state of being connected; relationship" according to Webster's Third New International Dictionary.

4. Quoted in J. I. Packer, *A Quest for Godliness: The Puritan Vision of the Christian Life* (Wheaton: Crossway, 1990), 262.

5. Alan Dunn, *Gospel Intimacy in a Godly Marriage: A Pursuit of Godly Romance* (North Bergen, NJ: Pillar and Ground Publications, 2009), 17.

6. "The Christian Directory," 2.1, dir. 9, in *The Practical Works of the Rev. Richard Baxter*, ed. William Orme (London: James Duncan, 1830), 4:30.

7. Gary Smalley, *Hidden Keys of the Loving, Lasting Marriage* (Grand Rapids: Zondervan, 1988), 325–26.

8. Smalley, *Hidden Keys*, 328.

9. William Gouge, *Of Domestical Duties* (1622; repr. n.p.: Puritan Reprints, 2006), 194 [3.4].

10. Baxter, "Christian Directory," 2.1, dir. 9, in *Works*, 4:30.

11. Baxter, "Christian Directory," 2.7, dir. 4, in *Works*, 4:122.

12. Baxter, "Christian Directory," 2.7, dir. 4, in *Works*, 4:122.

13. Cf. Joel R. Beeke, *Living for God's Glory: An Introduction to Calvinism* (Lake Mary, FL: Reformation Trust, 2008), 323–24.

14. Gary Thomas, *Sacred Marriage* (Grand Rapids: Zondervan, 2000), 202.

15. Remember that until modern times people did not marry for love. Marriage was much more a political, legal, and economic institution, bound up with notions of class and caste, the need to protect estates and inheritances, and the desire to acquire and increase wealth, prestige, and influence. Contractual marriage was the norm since ancient times. The common idea was that love, if you sought it, would come in time after you were married. When it failed to do so, seeking romance, love, and

pleasure from persons other than your marriage partner was more or less expected and winked at, if not encouraged. A man of wealth might buy his wife a slave to satisfy her desires, just as he kept one for himself. Potiphar's wife was no doubt shocked when Joseph objected to what she likely regarded as a fairly normal practice for women of her position in life.

16. Leland Ryken, *Worldly Saints: The Puritans As They Really Were* (Grand Rapids: Zondervan, 1986), 51.

17. *Matthew Henry's Commentary on the Whole Bible* (Peabody, MA: Hendrickson, 1991), 3:671 [Proverbs 5:15–23].

18. Ed and Gaye Wheat, *Intended for Pleasure*, 3rd ed. (Old Tappan, NJ: Revell, 1997).

19. Gary Chapman, *Covenant Marriage* (Nashville: Broadman and Holman, 2003), 190.

20. Consider the mob seeking to "know" (rape) Lot's visitors in Genesis 19:6.

21. Compare the (non-sexual) relational sense of "know" in Genesis 18:19 and Psalm 1:6.

22. On these physical and social differences between men and women, see Gregg Johnson, "Biological Basis for Gender-Specific Behavior," in *Recovering Biblical Manhood and Womanhood*, ed. John Piper and Wayne Grudem (Wheaton: Crossway, 1991), 282–85.

23. Willard F. Harley, Jr., *His Needs, Her Needs: Building an Affair-Proof Marriage* (Grand Rapids: Baker, 1994).

24. C. J. Mahaney, *Sex, Romance, and the Glory of God* (Wheaton: Crossway, 2004), 28. While I appreciate Mahaney's wisdom in this principle, I disagree with his Christless approach to the Song of Solomon.

25. Chapman, *Covenant Marriage*, 184–88.

26. Some Greek manuscripts omit "benevolence" but retain "duty." The debt owed between spouses is one of kindness, good will, and compassion. It is a cruel man or woman who insists on sex simply because "it's your duty to have sex with me."

27. Richard Steele, "What are duties of husbands and wives towards each other?" in *Puritan Sermons 1659–1689* (Wheaton: Richard Owen Roberts, 1981), 2:275.

28. William Gouge, *Of Domestical Duties* (1622; repr., Pensacola, FL: Puritan Reprints, 2006), 161 [2/2.9].
29. Henry, *Commentary on the Whole Bible*, 3:671 [Proverbs 5:15–23].
30. Gouge, *Of Domestical Duties*, 158 [2/2.4].
31. Tim and Beverly LaHaye, *The Act of Marriage: The Beauty of Sexual Love* (Grand Rapids: Zondervan, 1976), 16.
32. *Westminster Confession of Faith* (Glasgow: Free Presbyterian Publications, 2003), 222.
33. Thomas Watson, *The Duty of Self-Denial* (Morgan, PA: Soli Deo Gloria, 1996), 33.
34. Watson, *The Duty of Self-Denial*, 30.
35. David Powlison, "Making All Things New: Restoring Pure Joy to the Sexually Broken," in *Sex and the Supremacy of Christ*, ed. John Piper and Justin Taylor (Wheaton: Crossway Books, 2005), 71.
36. Powlison, "Making All Things New," in *Sex and the Supremacy of Christ*, 70.
37. R. C. Sproul, *Intimate Marriage* (Phillipsburg, NJ: P&R Publishing, 2003), 129.
38. Thomas, *Sacred Marriage*, 208.
39. "Form for the Confirmation of Marriage," *The Psalter*, 156.
40. Steele, "Duties of Husbands and Wives," in *Puritan Sermons*, 2:276.
41. Thomas, *Sacred Marriage*, 216.
42. Steele, "Duties of Husbands and Wives," in *Puritan Sermons*, 2:276.
43. Gouge, *Of Domestical Duties*, 260 [4.11].
44. Gouge, *Of Domestical Duties*, 260 [4.11].
45. Edward Taylor and John Winthrop, quoted in Ryken, *Worldly Saints*, 50.
46. Gouge, *Of Domestical Duties*, 161 [2/2.9].
47. Thomas, *Sacred Marriage*, 218.

CruciformPress

Books of about 100 pages
Clear, inspiring, gospel-centered

We like to keep it simple. So we publish short, clear, useful, inexpensive books for Christians and other curious people. Books that make sense and are easy to read, even as they tackle serious subjects.

We do this because the good news of Jesus Christ—the gospel—is the only thing that actually explains why this world is so wonderful and so awful all at the same time. Even better, the gospel applies to every single area of life, and offers real answers that aren't available from any other source.

In other words, the gospel changes everything.

Some of our authors are well known as writers, speakers, pastors, or bloggers. Others are new to the scene. Every one of them has something important and special to say, and says it well.

These are books you can afford, enjoy, finish easily, benefit from, and remember. Check us out and see. Then join us as part of a publishing revolution that's good news for the gospel, the church, and the world.

CruciformPress.com

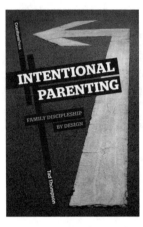

Intentional Parenting
Family Discipleship by Design

by Tad Thompson

The Big Picture and a Simple Plan — That's What You Need to Do Family Discipleship Well

This book will allow you to take all the sermons, teachings, and exhortations you have received on the topic of family discipleship, make sense of it, and put it to use.

"As parents, we know God has given us the responsibility to train our children in his ways. But many parents don't know where or how to start. Tad has done us all a favor by identifying seven key categories of biblical teaching we can utilize in teaching our children godly truth and principles. This easy-to-follow plan will help any parent put the truth of God's Word into their children's hearts."

Kevin Ezell, President, North American Mission Board, Southern Baptist Convention; father of six

"Here is a practical page-turner that encourages fathers to engage the hearts of their families with truth and grace. In an age when truth is either ignored or despised, it is refreshing to see a book written for ordinary fathers who want their families to be sanctified by the truth. Thompson writes with a grace which reminds us that parenting flows from the sweet mercies of Christ."

Joel Beeke, President, Puritan Reformed Theological Seminary

"Need an introductory text to the topic of discipling children? Here is a clear, simple book on family discipleship, centered on the gospel rather than human successes or external behaviors."

James M. Hamilton, Associate Professor of Biblical Theology, The Southern Baptist Theological Seminary

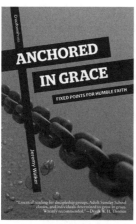

Anchored in Grace
Fixed Truths for Humble Faith

by Jeremy Walker

Clear truths from Scripture...

**Central. Humbling. Saving.
Comforting. God-glorifying.**

Get Anchored.

86 pages
bit.ly/ANCHRD

"Rarely does the title of a book so clearly represent its contents as does this one. With brevity and precision, Jeremy Walker sets forth God's work of salvation in the believer from beginning to end. In a day when there is so much confusion regarding even the most fundamental truths of redemption, this concise yet comprehensive work is a clear beacon of light to guide the seeker and to instruct and comfort the believer."
Paul David Washer, Director, HeartCry Missionary Society

"As a pastor, I am always looking for a book that is brief, simple, and biblical in its presentation of the God-exalting doctrines of grace to put into the hands of believers. I think my search is now over!"
Conrad Mbewe, African Christian University, Lusaka, Zambia

"Crisp, clear, concise, and biblical, Walker's book offers up the doctrines of God's grace in a manner persuasive to the mind and powerful to the heart."
Dr. Joel R. Beeke, Pres., Puritan Reformed Theological Seminary

"A sure-footed journey...a trusted guide. Reading this book will both thrill and convict, challenge and confirm. Essential reading for discipleship groups, Adult Sunday School classes, and individuals determined to grow in grace. Warmly recommended."
Derek W. H. Thomas, Professor, Reformed Theological Seminary

Licensed to Kill
A Field Manual for Mortifying Sin

by Brian G. Hedges

Your soul is a war zone.

Know your enemy.

Learn to fight.

101 pages
bit.ly/L2Kill

"Are there things you hate that you end up doing anyway? Have you tried to stop sinning in certain areas of your life, only to face defeat over and over again? If you're ready to get serious about sin patterns in your life—ready to put sin to death instead of trying to manage it—this book outlines the only strategy that works. This is a book I will return to and regularly recommend to others."

Bob Lepine, Co-Host, FamilyLife Today

"Rather than aiming at simple moral reformation, *Licensed to Kill* aims at our spiritual transformation. Like any good field manual, this one focuses on the most critical information regarding our enemy, and gives practical instruction concerning the stalking and killing of sin. This is a theologically solid and helpfully illustrated book that holds out the gospel confidence of sin's ultimate demise."

Joe Thorn, pastor and author, Note to Self: The Discipline of Preaching to Yourself

"Read this 'field-manual' and you will discover that you have a monstrous and aggressive antagonist who is aiming to annihilate you. It's your duty to fight back! Brian has given us a faithful, smart, Word-centered guide to help us identify and form a battle plan for mortally wounding the enemy of indwelling sin."

Wes Ward, Revive Our Hearts

Hit List
Taking Aim at the SevenDeadly Sins

by Brian G, Hedges

Pride, envy, wrath, sloth, greed, gluttony, lust: Not just corrupting vices, but gateway sins leading to countless others. Learn how to take aim at each one. Reach for holiness.

*112 pp.
Learn more at bit.ly/HITLIST-7*

"*Hit List* is a great book! Hedges brings the historic framework of the seven deadly sins into the 21st century. Brian's reading and research into historic Christian theology enriches this readable and thoroughly biblical examination and treatment of 'the big seven.'"
Tedd Tripp, author, conference speaker

"Satan destroys by cloaking his schemes in darkness. *Hit List* is a blazing floodlight—both convicting and gleaming with gospel clarity. For the Christian soldier eager to win the daily war against sin, *Hit List* is a welcome field manual."
Alex Crain, Editor, Christianity.com

"If you've ever heard you shouldn't envy (or get angry or lust or ...), but you don't know exactly what those sins look like in your everyday life—let alone the cure—then *Hit List* is for you. Brian has done his research, and I'm personally grateful for his insights on what's at the root of specific sins I deal with...and how I can break free. Read, repent, and live free!"
Paula Hendricks, Editorial Manager, Revive Our Hearts

"With characteristic depth, Brian unpacks an ancient formulation of our soul-sickness, while giving us the antidote of grace and gospel."
Del Fehsenfeld III, Senior Editor, Revive magazine

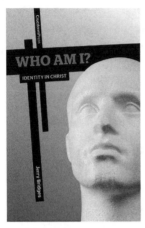

Who Am I?
Identity in Christ

by Jerry Bridges

Jerry Bridges unpacks Scripture to give the Christian eight clear, simple, interlocking answers to one of the most essential questions of life.

91 pages
bit.ly/WHOAMI

"Jerry Bridges' gift for simple but deep spiritual communication is fully displayed in this warm-hearted, biblical spelling out of the Christian's true identity in Christ."

J. I. Packer, *Theological Editor*, ESV Study Bible; *author*, Knowing God, A Quest for Godliness, Concise Theology

"I know of no one better prepared than Jerry Bridges to write *Who Am I?* He is a man who knows who he is in Christ and he helps us to see succinctly and clearly who we are to be. Thank you for another gift to the Church of your wisdom and insight in this book."

R.C. Sproul, *founder, chairman, president, Ligonier Ministries; executive editor,* Tabletalk *magazine; general editor,* The Reformation Study Bible

"*Who Am I?* answers one of the most pressing questions of our time in clear gospel categories straight from the Bible. This little book is a great resource to ground new believers and remind all of us of what God has made us through faith in Jesus. Thank the Lord for Jerry Bridges, who continues to provide the warm, clear, and biblically balanced teaching that has made him so beloved to this generation of Christians."

Richard D. Phillips, *Senior Minister, Second Presbyterian Church, Greenville, SC*

The Two Fears
Tremble Before God Alone
by Chris Poblete

**You can fear God...
or everything else.**

**Only one fear brings life and hope,
wisdom and joy.**

Fear wisely.

92 pages   bit.ly/2Fears

"We are too scared. And we aren't scared enough. Reading this book
will prompt you to seek in your own life the biblical tension between
'fear not' and 'fear God.'"

Russell D. Moore, Dean, Southern Baptist Theological Seminary

"An importantly counter-cultural book, moving us beyond a
homeboy God we could fist-bump to a holy God we can worship.
The Two Fears helps us recover a biblical fear of God and all the awe,
repentance, and freedom from self-centered fears that go with it. An
awesome resource!"

Dr. Thaddeus Williams, professor, Biola University

"In this practical and very readable book, Chris Poblete shows how
both the absence of true fear and the presence of 'unholy [false] fear'
stem from an absence of a knowledge of the awesome God of the
Bible, and that, in meeting him, we discover the real dimensions of
creational existence and the wonderful benefits of living in fear and
deep respect before him, freed from the '[false] fear of men.'"

**Peter Jones, Ph.D., TruthXchange; Scholar-in-Residence and
Adjunct Professor, Westminster Seminary in California**

"I commend this book to you: it will fuel your worship and empower
your discipleship."

Gabe Tribbett, Christ's Covenant Church, Winona Lake, IA

JOY!—A Bible Study on
Philippians for Women

FAITH: A Bible Study on
James for Women

bit.ly/JoyStudy

bit.ly/FaithStudy

Inductive Bible studies for women by Keri Folmar
endorsed by...

Kathleen Nielson is author of the *Living Word Bible Studies*; Director of Women's Initiatives, The Gospel Coalition; and wife of Niel, who served as President of Covenant College from 2002 to 2012.

Diane Schreiner – wife of professor, author, and pastor Tom Schreiner, and mother of four grown children – has led women's Bible studies for more than 20 years.

Connie Dever is author of *The Praise Factory* children's ministry curriculum and wife of Pastor Mark Dever, President of 9 Marks Ministries

Kristie Anyabwile, holds a history degree from NC State University, and is married to Thabiti, Senior Pastor of First Baptist Church, Grand Cayman, and a Council Member for The Gospel Coalition.

Gloria Furman is a pastor's wife in the Middle East and author of *Glimpses of Grace* and *Treasuring Christ When Your Hands Are Full.*

The Company We Keep
In Search of Biblical Friendship

by Jonathan Holmes
Foreword by Ed Welch

Biblical friendship is deep, honest, pure, tranparent, and liberating.

It is also attainable.

112 pages
bit.ly/B-Friend

"Jonathan Holmes has the enviable ability to say a great deal in a few words. Here is a wonderful primer on the nature of biblical friendship—what it means and why it matters."
Alistair Begg, Truth for Life; Senior Pastor, Parkside Church

"Jonathan has succeeded in giving us a picture of how normal, daily, biblical friend-ships can be used by God to mold us into the likeness of Christ. If you want a solid, fresh way of re-thinking all of your relationships, read this book."
Dr. Tim S. Lane, co-author, How People Change

"A robust and relevant GPS for intentional and vulnerable gospel-centered friendships....a great book not only for individuals, but also for small groups...a signifi-cant contribution to the Kingdom."
Robert W. Kellemen, Exec. Dir., Biblical Counseling Coalition

"Short. Thoughtful. Biblical. Practical. I'm planning to get my friends to read this book so we can transform our friendships."
Deepak Reju, Pastor of Biblical Counseling, Capitol Hill Baptist

"Filled with answers that are equally down-to-earth, nitty-gritty, and specific....taking us where we need to go with warmth and wisdom."
Wesley Hill, author, Washed and Waiting

Getting Back in the Race
The Cure for Backsliding

by Joel R. Beeke

Backsliding is the worst thing that can happen to anyone claiming faith in Jesus.

Find out why. Learn the diagnosis. Experience the cure.

"This book is a masterpiece, and I do not say that lightly. This excellent work, so helpfully spiced with quotations from the Puritans, needs to be read over and over again. I heartily commend it."
Martin Holdt, pastor; editor, Reformation Africa South

"Joel Beeke's characteristic clarity, biblical fidelity, and unflinching care as to detail and pastoral wisdom is obvious on every page. This book is an honest and sometimes chilling exposition of the seriousness of backsliding; at the same time, it unfailingly breathes the air of grace and hope. Timely and judicious."
Derek W. H. Thomas, First Presbyterian Church, Columbia, SC; Editorial Director, Alliance of Confessing Evangelicals

"'Don't settle for being a spiritual shrimp,' argues Dr. Beeke. The pity is that too many modern Christians are opting for shrimpishly small degrees of grace. Indwelling sin drags the careless believer down into guilty backsliding. This book is a prescription for the believer who feels his guilt."
Maurice Roberts, former editor, Banner of Truth _magazine_

"Dr. Beeke outlines the best means of bringing balm and healing to the backslidden soul. Highly recommended."
Michael Haykin, Professor, Southern Baptist Theo. Sem.

After They are Yours
The Grace and Grit of Adoption

by Brian Borgman
Foreword by Dan Cruver

This is about the "other side" of adoption, the difficult realities that are not often discussed. What do you do when it's hard to hope? Here is a story of adoption that's real, raw, redemptive, and edifying.

102 pages
bit.ly/AfterThey

"A compelling story about saying *yes* to God and then watching the Father shape and redeem his sons and daughters through love, grace, and mercy."
Kelly Rosati, V.P. Community Outreach, Focus on the Family

"The decision to adopt is heroic. The reality is often hard. This book does not sugar coat the sacrifice that comes standard with adoption. It will help those considering adoption count the cost. And it will provide encouragement and help for parents who have already welcomed a child into their forever family."
Bob Lepine, Co-Host, FamilyLife Today

"It's all here — joy, hurt, and longing. And this is precisely what we most need: truth-telling that plunges beyond cliche and facade to speak of both the beauty and the brokenness that so often come woven together in adoption, all of it wrapped round by God's limitless grace."
Jedd Medefind, President, Christian Alliance for Orphans

"Brian Borgman lets us step into his family's experience as he unashamedly shares the joys and difficulties of their adoption story. Pain and loss are an inescapable part of every adoption, and Borgman points us to the gospel that provides both the framework and the fuel families will need for the challenges... an excellent resource."
Stephen Story, Executive Director of Covenant Care Services

Grieving, Hope and Solace
When a Loved One Dies in Christ

by Albert N. Martin

**There is comfort for the grief.
There are answers to the questions.
The Bible does offer hope, solace,
healing, and confidence.**

**Pastor Albert Martin has been
there.**

"This tender book by a much-loved pastor, written after the death of
his beloved wife, offers comfort to those in tears. A rare guidebook to
teach us how to grieve with godliness, it is relevant to us all – if not for
today, then no doubt for tomorrow."

Maurice Roberts, former editor, Banner of Truth magazine

"Albert N. Martin is a seasoned pastor, skilled teacher, and gifted writer
who has given us a priceless treasure in this book. All who read these
pages will, unquestionably, be pointed to Christ and find themselves
greatly helped."

Steve Lawson, Christ Fellowship Baptist Church, Mobile, AL

"Like turning the corner and being met by a glorious moonrise, or
discovering a painter or musician who touches us in the deepest
recesses of our being—this little book by Pastor Al Martin has been
such an experience for me. Whether you are a pastor or counselor,
one who is experiencing the pangs of grief, or a member of the
church who wants to be useful to others, you need to read this book."

Joseph Pipa, President, Greenville Presbyterian Theo. Sem.

"Personal tenderness and biblical teaching in a sweet book of comfort. Buy it and give it away, but make sure to get a copy for yourself."

Dr. Joel R. Beeke, President, Puritan Reformed Theo. Sem.

Torn to Heal
God's Good Purpose in Suffering
by Mike Leake

**Recieve comfort for today.
Be prepared to for tomorrow.**

*87 pages
Learn more at bit.ly/TORN2H*

"The most concise, readable, and helpful theology of suffering I've come across. The content, length, and tone is just perfect for those who are in the furnace of affliction screaming 'Why?'"
Dr. David Murray, Puritan Reformed Theological Seminary

"Mike Leake has taken the ugliness of suffering, turned it over in his capable hands, and shown God's goodness and faithfulness in the midst. More than simple encouragement, it is a handbook of scriptural truths about Who God is and how He sustains."
Lore Ferguson writes for Gospel Coalition, CBMW, and more

"A gospel-driven path between dualism that acts as if God has lost control of his world and fatalism/stoicism that tries to bury pain beneath emotionless acceptance of whatever happens. The result is a brief but potent primer on the purpose of suffering."
Timothy Paul Jones, Southern Baptist Theological Seminary

"Explores God's redemptive purposes in human suffering in a concise, biblical and authentic way. Mike shuns cliches and platitudes to help the reader put life's hardships into divine perspective and to endure in Christ's strength. It is a must-read for Christians in distress."
Dave Miller, Second Vice-President, Southern Baptist Convention

Knowable Word
Helping Ordinary People Learn to Study the Bible

by Peter Krol
Foreword by Tedd Tripp

Observe...Interpret...Apply

Simple concepts at the heart of good Bible study. Learn the basics in a few minutes—gain skills for a lifetime. The spiritual payoff is huge...ready?

108 pages   bit.ly/Knowable

"Peter Krol has done us a great service by writing the book Knowable Word. It is valuable for those who have never done in-depth Bible study and a good review for those who have. I look forward to using this book to improve my own Bible study.'"
Jerry Bridges, author, The Pursuit of Holiness, and many more

"It is hard to over-estimate the value of this tidy volume. It is clear and uncomplicated. No one will be off-put by this book. It will engage the novice and the serious student of Scripture. It works as a solid read for individuals or as an exciting study for a small group."
Tedd Tripp, pastor and author (from the Foreword)

"At the heart of *Knowable Word* is a glorious and crucial conviction: that understanding the Bible is not the preserve of a few, but the privilege and joy of all God's people. Peter Krol's book demystifies the process of reading God's Word and in so doing enfranchises the people of God. I warmly encourage you to read it. "
Dr. Tim Chester, The Porterbrook Network

"Here is an excellent practical guide to interpreting the Bible. Krol has thought through, tested, and illustrated in a clear, accessible way basic steps in interpreting the Bible, and made everything available in a way that will encourage ordinary people to deepen their own study."
Vern Poythress, Westminster Theological Seminary

Brass Heavens
Reasons for Unanswered Prayer

by Paul Tautges

Does it ever seem like God is not listening?

Scripture offers six clear reasons why your prayers may go unanswered.

Learn what they are and what you can do about it.

112 pages   bit.ly/BRASS-H

"Paul Tautges scatters the darkness of doubt. He blends biblical teaching with practical illustrations to challenge and comfort us when the heavens seem as brass. Read this to revive your prayers, to melt the heavens, and to increase your answers."
David Murray, Puritan Reformed Theological Seminary

"Some things in the Scriptures are conveniently ignored...but this book will not let us continue to bury Scripture's clear teaching, or continue to ignore the ongoing rebellions, unrelinquished resentments, and unconfessed sins in our lives that may be hindering our prayers."
Nancy Guthrie, author, **Seeing Jesus in the Old Testament**

"Both motivating and convicting....Read and obey for the sake of your future, your family, and the work of God in the world."
Jim Elliff, President, Christian Communicators Worldwide

"Like the Scriptures, Paul Tautges does not leave us in the pit of despair, but shows that where sin abounds, grace superabounds—there are biblical pathways for dealing with our role in unanswered prayers and for responding humbly to God's affectionate sovereignty."
Bob Kellemen, Executive Dir., Biblical Counseling Coalition

"But God…"
The Two Words at the Heart of the Gospel

by Casey Lute

**Just two words.
Understand their use in Scripture,
and you will never be the same.**

100 pages
bit.ly/ButGOD

"Keying off of nine occurrences of "But God" in the English Bible, Casey Lute ably opens up Scripture in a manner that is instructive, edifying, encouraging, and convicting. This little book would be useful in family or personal reading, or as a gift to a friend. You will enjoy Casey's style, you will have a fresh view of some critical Scripture, and your appreciation for God's mighty grace will be deepened."

Dan Phillips, Pyromaniacs blog, author of The World-Tilting Gospel (forthcoming from Kregel)

"A refreshingly concise, yet comprehensive biblical theology of grace that left this reader more in awe of the grace of God."

Aaron Armstrong, BloggingTheologically.com

""Casey Lute reminds us that nothing is impossible with God, that we must always reckon with God, and that God brings life out of death and joy out of sorrow."

Thomas R. Schreiner, Professor of New Testament Interpretation, The Southern Baptist Theological Seminary

"A mini-theology that will speak to the needs of every reader of this small but powerful book. Read it yourself and you will be blessed. Give it to a friend and you will be a blessing."

William Varner, Prof. of Biblical Studies, The Master's College